# NIAGARA
## ON-THE-LAKE
### ITS HERITAGE AND ITS FESTIVAL

Ronald J. Dale

Photography by Dwayne Coon

Foreword by Christopher Newton

JAMES LORIMER & COMPANY LTD., PUBLISHERS
TORONTO, 1999

© 1999 Ronald J. Dale

James Lorimer & Company Ltd. acknowledges the support
of the Department of Canadian Heritage and the Ontario
Arts Council in the development of writing and publishing
in Canada. We acknowledge the support of the Canada
Council for the Arts for our publishing program.

Canadä

Cover: Dwayne Coon

Cataloguing in Publication Data

Dale, Ronald J., 1951-
  Niagara-on-the-Lake: Its Heritage and Its Festival

Includes index.
ISBN 1-55028-647-1

1. Niagara-on-the-Lake (Ont.) — History. 2. Niagara-on-
the-Lake (Ont.) — Tours. I. Title

FC3099.N54D34 1999                971.3'38
C99-930334-1
F1059.5.N5D34 1999

James Lorimer & Company Ltd., Publishers
35 Britain Street
Toronto, Ontario
M5A 1R7
Printed and bound in Canada.

# CONTENTS

# FOREWORD

It's very daring of Ron Dale to write a history of Niagara-on-the-Lake. It is daring because there are so many of us who have ideas about writing either a guide or a memoir or a history of this seductive town. And whenever someone like Ron Dale actually does it, then we would-be authors naturally compare the achievement with the guides and histories that stay firmly lodged in the feather beds of our lazy imaginations. "Ho, ho," we mutter, "he's left out the story of the runaway engine." Or we dive for another history to check a date which seems questionable. (I did this with a Shaw fact and found that my memory had played me false and that Ron Dale was right.)

My own history of Niagara-on-the-Lake I conceive as being literary and horticultural. I'd be writing about Mrs. Simcoe's literary evenings, about the garrison theatricals, about William Kirby and *The Golden Dog*, about Dickens looking at our little town as he passed us on the packet boat from Queenston to Toronto, about the Prince of Wales's entourage of diarists, about Peter Tchaikovsky looking down river from the Falls, about Malcolm Lowry, and I might even be able to get Bernard Shaw in there somehow. He'd probably heard of us—after all he'd heard or

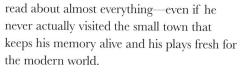

read about almost everything—even if he never actually visited the small town that keeps his memory alive and his plays fresh for the modern world.

The horticultural side of my book wouldn't touch so much on the orchards and new vineyards as on the gardens. There are so many hidden gardens in Niagara. A gap in a hedge, an open gate, can offer glimpses of paradise on the most unexpected streets. And the joy of discovery is not confined to the plants, particularly roses, which flourish in our rich clay soil. No, part of the delight comes from actually digging in our gardens. I keep two plastic flower pots by me as I dig. One is for stones, roots, anything I want to throw away, the

other is for the treasures. I have lots of bits of clay pipe, many fragments of pottery with lovely Victorian patterns in blue or pale mauve, a bayonet, an Edward VII nickel, two railway spikes, and what could be an arrowhead. My neighbour actually dug up a cannon ball.

People have lived here for a very long time. They have told stories about the place and they have grown food and flowers here. We've suffered through a war and, incidentally, when the war was over and people thought things would get better, they suffered through the year without a summer. No crops ripened and fruit died on the trees because the sun was blotted out when the greatest vol-canic eruption in modern history darkened the skies around the world. Mount Tambora exploded in 1815 and every farm and garden in Niagara-on-the-Lake failed in the following year.

The bell at St. Mark's has rung out for deaths and famines, for victories in the Crimea, the South African War, two world wars. We were protected by distance and committed by nature to try to achieve that state of paradise that we found in our own back yards. Ron Dale has given us a history that makes me happy to live in such a blessed spot.

Christopher Newton, C.M.

*Fife and drum corps, Fort George*

# INTRODUCTION

*210 John Street*

The beautiful and historic town of Niagara-on-the-Lake has been known by many names over the years. The first recorded name of the area was a native word, *Onguiaahra*, which was eventually simplified to Niagara. It has also been known as West Niagara, Butlersburg, Lenox, Newark and finally Niagara-on-the-Lake.

Niagara-on-the-Lake is a town of firsts. It was the first capital of Ontario, had the first newspaper, the first Masonic lodge, the first agricultural society and the first library, and was where the Law Society of Upper Canada was founded. It was here that the first anti-slavery legislation in the British Empire was passed.

With well-restored buildings and charming streetscapes,

interesting historic sites and museums and more than its share of ghosts, the town is a living historic community, a place where the past hovers just below the surface. Residents tilling their gardens and builders excavating homes will inevitably churn up the relics deposited over the years by previous residents — flint projectile points thousands of years old, musket balls fired in the fierce fighting of the War of 1812, ashes from the razing of the first town by enemy soldiers, elegant ceramics from the Victorian age and a treasure of artifacts discarded or lost by the thousands who have left their mark on the town. People have lived here, thriving in the gentle Niagara climate and enjoying the beauty of its natural setting, for the past ten millennia.

Niagara-on-the-Lake has seen soaring success and dismal depression. The first capital of the new Province of Upper Canada (Ontario), the rapidly growing town suffered when the capital was "temporarily" moved to York (Toronto) in 1796. It was captured, occupied and finally completely burned by American forces during the War of 1812. Rebuilt, the town again prospered but experienced a severe economic depression following the construction of the second Welland Canal in the 1840s. Recovering again, the town became a very popular tourist destination in the late nineteenth century, but this ended with World War I and the Great Depression of the 1930s. After World War II, Niagara-on-the-Lake suffered from high unemployment and a slow economy. The sad state of its economy ultimately was its saviour. Few could afford to

enjoy the postwar building boom occurring in other towns, and while elsewhere the postwar generation was tearing down the tired old "eyesores" in their municipalities to make way for smart new concrete block and angel-stone bungalows, the people of Niagara-on-the-Lake made do with their century-old, drafty and sometimes rundown houses and stores.

*Statue of George Bernard Shaw, Queen Street*

Niagara-on-the-Lake may not have had much money, but it certainly had its history and incomparable location, along with some forward-looking people. Some resources are priceless.

In the late 1950s, a few people restored their old buildings, revealing them for the gems that they were. A few years later, a group of residents established a summer theatre program based on the works of George Bernard Shaw. The mix of heritage and culture touched a chord and, within two decades, the town was transformed. Its treasury of early nineteenth-century buildings was carefully restored, the professional Shaw Festival was firmly established and thousands of tourists converged on the town. Today, Niagara-on-the-Lake is booming as it never has before, with over three million visitors sharing the town with its 5,000 inhabitants each year. Visitors are attracted by the elegant shops, hotels and restaurants, the wineries, vineyards and fruit orchards and the carefully restored buildings and fascinating historic sites of the old town.

# MAPS

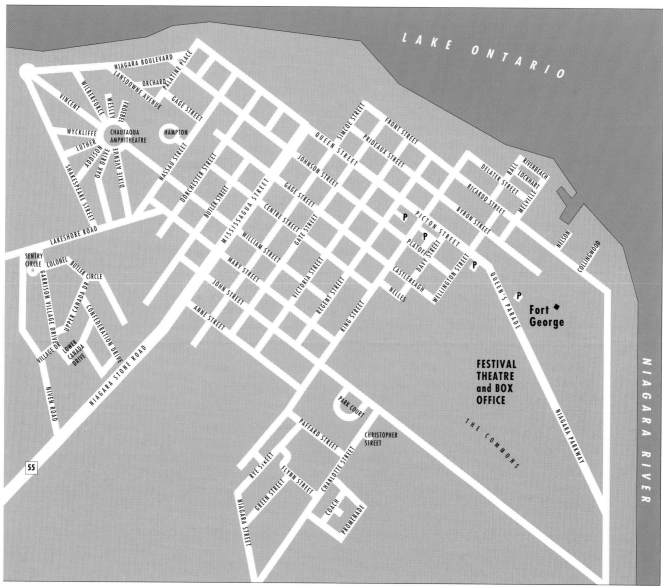

*Niagara-on-the-Lake*

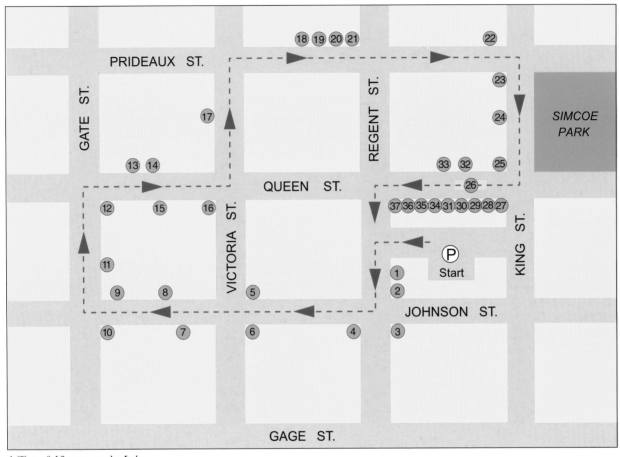

*A Tour of Niagara-on-the-Lake*

1 The Angel Inn, 46 Market St.
2 Lawn Bowling Green
3 Barker Hall, 46 Johnson St.
4 Eckersley House, 58 Johnson St.
5 Post House, 95 Johnson St.
6 Vanderlip House, 96 Johnson St.
7 The Varey House,
   105 Johnson St.
8 Varey's Terrace, 117–
   119 Johnson St
9 Greenlees House, 135 Johnson St.
10 Ralph Clement House,
   144 Johnson St.
11 McMonigle House, 240 Gate St.
12 Gate House Hotel, 142 Queen St.
13 Candy Safari, 135 Queen St.
14 Angie Strauss Art Gallery,
   129 Queen St.

15 Customs House, 126 Queen St.
16 McLelland's West End Store,
   106 Queen St.
17 Wilson-Kent House,
   175 Victoria St.
18 Davidson-Campbell House,
   87 Prideaux St.
19 Dobie-Campbell House,
   83 Prideaux St.
20 Kerr's Demeath House,
   69 Prideaux St.
21 Promenade House,
   55 Prideaux St.
22 McKee House, 18 Prideaux St.
23 Masonic Hall, 153 King St.
24 Preservation Gallery, 177 King St.
25 The Niagara Apothecary,
   5 Queen St.

26 The War Memorial Clock Tower
27 Squire Clements Block,
   4-8 Queen St.
28 Firehall, 10 Queen St.
29 Loyalist Village, 12 Queen St.
30 Sign of the Pineapple,
   16 Queen St.
31 Liquor Store, 20 Queen St.
32 7–9 Queen St.
33 13–15 Queen St.
34 The Courthouse, 26 Queen St.
35 Sherlock Block 34–36 Queen St.
36 The Irish Shop, 38–42 Queen St.
37 Old Niagara Bookshop,
   44 Queen St.

# 1

# A Tour of Niagara-on-the-Lake

Any street in the Old Town takes a visitor back through time, past buildings constructed over the last 180 years. There are dozens of historic structures, from the simple to the grandiose, each with a story to tell. Most have been restored to their original appearance. The following presents one simple tour out of dozens of possible routes.

From the courthouse parking lot proceed along Market Street to Regent Street.

*Lawn Bowling Green*

*The Angel Inn*

**The Angel Inn, 46 Market Street, circa 1825** – The Angel Inn, originally known as the Sign of the Angel, has served travellers for the past 175 years. It now features a wide selection of beers and ales along with the wines of the Niagara Region. The Angel is reputed to be haunted by the ghost of a War of 1812 soldier who becomes agitated only when the Union Jack does not fly above the door of the inn.

***Lawn Bowling Green, circa 1920s*** – After the closing of the Queen's Royal Hotel in 1925 and its lawn bowling facilities, this became the only lawn bowling green in town. Many local residents enjoy a quiet summer game of "bowls".

Turn on to Johnson Street.

***Barker Hall, 46 Johnson Street, circa 1831*** – Barker Hall is typical of many houses in Ontario, with a central doorway flanked by a parlour and a keeping room inside, and a central staircase rising from the front door. An unusual feature, seen in a few houses in Niagara-on-the-Lake, is the off-centre doorway to allow for a larger

*Barker Hall*

rare dated keystone over the door is a boon for present-day historians. The house has this name since it was one of Niagara's early post offices.

***Vanderlip House, 96 Johnson Street, circa 1816*** – The Vanderlip House was one of the first built after the War of 1812 to replace the houses burned in 1813. It was built as a one-and-a-half-storey structure, taxed at the time of construction at the same rate as a one-storey house — considerably less than the tax on two full storeys. The windows on the second level at the front of

*Post House*

the house are later additions. For many years this house was rumoured to be much older, one of the few survivors of the War of 1812.

room to the right of the door. This makes the façade asymmetrical in appearance.

***Eckersley House, 58 Johnson Street, circa 1833*** – Eckersley House shows the attention to detail lavished on buildings by early craftsmen. Note the impressive doorway with sidelights and fanlights that have been carefully restored.

*Eckersley House*

***Post House, 95 Johnson Street, circa 1835*** – The red brick building on the right was built by mason James Blair, who maintained a brickyard near the house. The structure stands as a good advertisement for Blair's brick supply business and his skill as a mason. Large windows make the building bright and airy. A relatively

*Vanderlip House*

*The Varey House*

**The Varey House, 105 Johnson Street, circa 1837 –** George Varey, the owner of this house, was listed as a tailor. He must have been very successful at his trade because he owned this substantial stucco house and the row house at 115–119 Johnson. The house is in the Regency style. The property remained in the Varey family from the period prior to the War of 1812 until 1899.

**Varey's Terrace, 117–119 Johnson Street, circa 1840s –** This red row house was built by entrepreneur George Varey to house workers of the Niagara Harbour and Dock Company. We are fortunate that a building with humble beginnings has survived and has been faithfully preserved.

**Greenlees House, 135 Johnson Street, circa 1822 –** Another very early "postwar" house, it shares an asymmetrical centre hallway plan with several other houses from the same period in the town's history. One wonders if the same builder was involved in their construction or if the owners simply liked the idea of having one larger room on the ground floor.

**Ralph Clement House, 144 Johnson Street, circa 1840s –** This substantial red brick home has the same type of generous window treatment as the Post House, built a few years earlier by mason James Blair. The Clement House was also likely built by Blair, using bricks from his supply yard.

Turn right on Gate Street.

*Varey's Terrace*

*Ralph Clement House*

*Greenlees House*

*McMonigle House*

*McMonigle House, 240 Gate Street, circa 1818 –* The McMonigle House is another of Niagara's earliest houses, built of frame and board following the War of 1812.

*Gate House Hotel, 142 Queen Street, circa 1900 –* On this site stood John Wilson's tavern, where the Law

*Angie Strauss Art Gallery*

Society of Upper Canada was founded in 1797, the year that the Provincial Legislature moved from Niagara to Toronto. Although the society was founded here, it was established in Toronto, where it still oversees Ontario's legal profession.

Turn right on Queen Street.

*Candy Safari, 135 Queen Street, circa 1835 –* This frame structure was built as a house and shop for shoemaker John Burns. The Gothic-Revival style building has served as a residence and place

*Customs House*

of business throughout its long history.

*Angie Strauss Art Gallery, 129 Queen Street, circa 1860s –* Artist Angie Strauss's gallery is one of four old town buildings dating from the period right after the American Civil War. Like 135 Queen Street and many other buildings in the town's business district it has served as both shop and residence.

*Candy Safari*

*Customs House, 126 Queen Street, circa 1825 –* Notice the coat of arms over the building on the other side of Queen Street. This marks the Customs House, which was built as a residence and government office. The early use of the Regency style for the structure shows that the government was at the cutting edge of design in the 1820s. It has been restored with a reconstructed coat of arms adorning its front façade.

*McLelland's West End Store, 106 Queen Street, circa 1835 –* With the town's rapidly growing population during the shipbuilding boom of the 1830s, this store with

*Gate House Hotel*

*McLelland's West End Store*

its Classic Revival gable front was built as a provisioner's — selling groceries, wines and spirits to residents and travellers. Notice the large painted "T" sign of the provisioner. The store was very successful, and in 1880 an extension was built beside it at 108 Queen Street. Both structures still house stores servicing residents and visitors and are superbly preserved examples of Niagara's commercial past.

Turn left on Victoria

***Wilson-Kent House, 177 Victoria Street, circa 1816 –*** This frame house was built for "Irish John" Wilson, a successful hotelier in Niagara. This five-bay building is a storey and a half in height, common in many early buildings when buildings of this size were taxed at the same rate as single

*Wilson-Kent House*

storey buildings. A full two storeys added to the tax bill.

Turn right on Prideaux Street

***Davidson-Campbell House, 87 Prideaux Street, circa 1845 –*** This interesting house, built during the first few years of Queen Victoria's long reign, was renovated later in the nineteenth century and several embellishments were added which make it unique. Among the building's

*Davidson-Campbell House*

*Promenade House*

ornamental elements are lacework frills, drops and finials along the eaves in a Gothic Revival style.

***Dobie-Campbell House, 83 Prideaux Street, circa 1835 –***
One of early Niagara's most skilled carpenters, John Davidson, likely built this frame house. Davidson worked on at least two of the town's churches, St. Andrew's and St. Vincent de Paul's, and several of his elaborate staircases continue to grace Niagara homes.

***Kerr's "Demeath" House, 69 Prideaux Street, circa 1815* –** Dr. Robert Kerr, staff surgeon of the British Indian Department during the War of 1812, built this house on the ruins of his first house which had been

burned by the retreating American army on December 10, 1813. The structure, of Flemish bond brickwork, preserves a great deal of the earliest moldings, mantlepieces and other embellishments inside.

*McKee House*

***Promenade House, 55 Prideaux Street, circa 1820* –**
This brick building, also of Flemish bond brickwork, served as one of Niagara's many inns. While it was built as a residence it was easily converted to a tavern by Innkeeper Richard Howard who had earlier owned the Angel Inn. The transom over the door retains its delicate Regency decorative elements.

***McKee House, 18 Prideaux Street, circa 1835* –** Alexander McKee, the owner of this house, was one of several schoolmasters in early Niagara. It retains

*Dobie-Campbell House*

*Kerr's "Demeath" House*

*Masonic Hall*

*The Niagara Apothecary*

*Preservation Gallery*

many of its original features, inside and out. Unlike most Niagara homes of the period, heating and cooking was not provided by fireplaces but by cast iron stoves which were becoming more common by the 1830s.

Turn right on King Street

**Masonic Hall, 153 King Street, circa 1816** – The Masonic Hall is reputed to have been built using rubble from the burned town in 1816. It served as a store, as the "stone" barracks and, since the 1860s, as the Masonic Temple. The Masonic lodge in Niagara goes back over 200 years, the first in Ontario. The original Temple was built near this site in the early 1790s long before the first church in the area was constructed. After their hall was burned in 1813, the masons met in various locations before finally taking over this building. Today the structure also serves as the busy Chamber of Commerce office where the vistor can pick up information or book a room in one of the town's many B&Bs or hotels.

**Preservation Gallery, 177 King Street, 1870s** – This large, beautifully restored house is a beautiful example of the decorative style which marks the height of the Victorian age. The central tower and Saracen roof are notable features. The building serves as the gallery for the art of Trish Romance and is as splendid inside as is the exterior and its gardens.

Turn right on Queen Street. The walker may choose to walk down either side of Queen to enjoy its historic stores.

**The Niagara Apothecary, 5 Queen Street, circa 1820** – The Apothecary building was a simple post-war structure until the 1850s when it was modified with the splendid italianate front preserved here today. This was an operating pharmacy for a century. It was one of the first buildings saved and restored through the efforts of the Niagara Foundation. It is refurnished to its Confederation period appearance with a selection of snake oil and cure-alls. A pharmacy museum is operated by the Ontario College of Pharmacy.

**The War Memorial Clock Tower, 1922 –**

In the middle of Queen Street is the tower built in 1922 as the town's War Memorial following World War I. It was rededicated after World War II to commemorate a new generation of Canadians who gave their lives for our freedom.

*Squire Clements Block*

*The War Memorial Clock Tower*

**Squire Clements Block, 4–8 Queen Street, circa 1835 –** In the 1830s King Street was becoming busier while Queen was established as the main business street. This block has storefronts on Queen and one corner store-

front to attract shoppers from any direction.

**Firehall, 10 Queen Street, circa 1911 –** This store was built by the Niagara fire brigade as their firehall in 1911. It has been commercial space for the past eight decades.

**Loyalist Village, 12 Queen Street, circa 1850 –** The store on this spot was built a few years after the completion of the court-house, fell on hard times during the early 1860s but has been

*Loyalist Village*

the site of thriving businesses for the past 120 years.

**Sign of the Pineapple, 16 Queen Street, circa 1830 –** The well-restored building which houses The Owl and the Pussycat has interesting carved pineapples on window frame details and over the door. These were symbols of hospitality and welcome, sentiments still proudly upheld by the shop.

*Firehall*

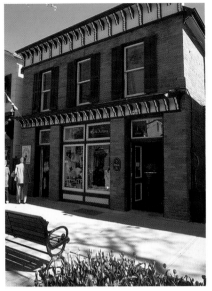

*7–9 Queen Street*

*13–15 Queen Street*

***Liquor Store, 20 Queen Street, circa 1817*** – This extremely early brick building began as a one storey structure. After the massive courthouse was completed in the 1840s, the building was expanded and a second storey added. It must be Ontario's most historic liquor store.

***Commercial Buildings, 7–9 Queen Street, circa 1890 and 1880*** – Beside the Apothecary, these buildings were constructed as Niagara's first tourism boom got underway in the last decades of the nineteenth century. The styles are very typical of commercial buildings in that time period and similar architecture can be seen in neighbouring Niagara area towns.

***13–15 Queen Street, circa 1860*** – A commercial block which some local historians feel may have been built as a residence is one of four buildings in the heritage district from the 1860s era. The early 1860s saw an economic downturn which slowed construction in the town.

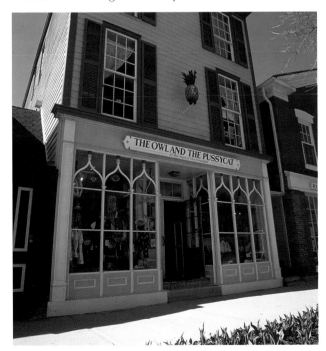

*Sign of the Pineapple*

*Liquor Store*

*The Courthouse*

*The Irish Shop*

***The Courthouse, 26 Queen Street, circa 1847*** – This magnificent public building, a National Historic Site, was constructed as the county seat of the Niagara District with court-rooms, meeting rooms and jail cells. When the county seat was moved to St. Catharines in 1862, resulting in an economic downturn in Niagara, the court-house became the town hall. It is also the site where the Shaw Festival was founded and it still houses the Court House Theatre of the Shaw. Notice the stone faces carved over the windows. Whether they are caricatures of persons of the time or completely whimsical is not known.

***Sherlock Block, 34–36 Queen Street, circa 1850*** – The Sherlock Block, actually two smaller buildings joined together, was contructed soon after the completion of the courthouse to take advantage of the many persons doing

*Sherlock Block*

business at that building. The high facade conceals the fact that it is two buildings and gives the structure height to prevent it from being overwhelmed by the massive courthouse.

***The Irish Shop, 38–42 Queen Street, circa 1840*** – Constructed as both a shop and residential space during the height of the shipbuilding era, this site like its neigh-bours on the block was originally built on land leased from the town.

***Old Niagara Bookshop, 44 Queen Street, circa 1981*** – The bookshop and its neigh-bour, the Glens of Scotland, are in a restored building on the site of the Alma and Daly buildings. The stores are faithful copies of historic buildings.

*Old Niagara Bookshop*

Turn left on Regent Street and you have returned to the beginning of the tour.

# 2

# THE EARLY HISTORY OF NIAGARA

Canada is often called a young country with a short history. The same cannot be said of the Niagara area where people have lived for the past ten millennia. The first hunters and gatherers adapted their lifestyles to changing ecological factors, and their society slowly evolved. By the time their descendants met the first Europeans to travel to this area 400 years ago, the Native people had developed very complex social and political organizations. Their descendants still live in the area.

*Representations of Paleo-Indians*

Groups of men, women and children came as itinerant hunters to the Niagara area and stayed.

These first Niagarans were a true stone-age or Paleolithic people known as "Paleo-Indians." Skilled hunters of caribou and other creatures of the boreal forest, they travelled in small groups, setting up temporary camps in their hunting grounds. All that has survived of these people are their carefully crafted stone knives, spear heads, scrapers and engravers and, occasionally, their mortal remains. Undoubtedly, their traditions were passed on through the generations and may form part of the traditional knowledge of Native people today.

## The First People

Ten thousand years ago in what is now Ontario, the great glaciers of the last ice age retreated north during a period of global warming. The land which had long been crushed under the incredible weight of ice began to rebound and the shorelines of the huge Lake Iroquois receded to form the present shape of Lake Ontario. Herds of caribou, mastodon, muskox and deer roamed the new spruce forests between lake and glacier and were hunted by humans.

The Paleo-Indian people slowly adapted their tools and lifestyles to the changing landscape and climate of Niagara. As the climate warmed, the forests gradually changed to mixed deciduous trees. The muskox and near-depleted caribou herds moved north as the boreal forest receded. The mastodon became extinct by about 7000 B.C., while more modern species — elk, bison, white-tailed deer, bear, rabbit and others — increased in numbers. The descendants of the Paleo-Indian people who lived in the long period from around 8000 B.C. to 1000 B.C., called the "Archaic" period by archaeologists, adapted their lifestyles, hunting methods and tools as the climate and game changed over those seven millennia.

The Archaic people refined the food-gathering activities of their ancestors and were skilled hunters of elk, deer, bison, beaver and bear as well as a variety of small game including rabbits, squirrels and birds. At some point, the bow and arrow and the atlatl, a spear-throwing stick, improved their hunting successes. These people also harvested the bounties of Lake Ontario, the Niagara River and the many streams in the area, gathering shellfish and catching fish with harpoons and fish hooks. During this period, the dog was domesticated to become an important part of Native life for the next several millennia.

## The Woodland People

About 3000 years ago, the people of Niagara learned the methods of manufacturing pottery. The use of pottery marks the beginning of the "Woodland" period, a designation given by archaeologists to describe this stage in the technological development of indigenous peoples in Ontario. In the period beginning around 1000 B.C. and continuing for the next several centuries, the early Woodland peoples did not live

*Representation of Woodland people*

much differently from their archaic ancestors but they did perfect the manufacture of pottery, which affected their methods of storing and cooking food. This period also marked the beginning of an increase in the population of Native people in Niagara.

*Stone pendant, Early Woodland period*

The early Woodland people were part of the "Meadowood Culture," which dates back to between 900 B.C. and 400 B.C. These people continued most of the trade networks of their ancestors, although they seem to have lost access to more distant trade. They became expert fishermen and used a variety of watercraft including elm-bark canoes on the inland waters. Their beautiful ground-stone gorgets, or chest ornaments, their polished birdstones, mysterious objects carved in the shape of birds, and tubular ceramic tobacco pipes survive as a testament to their artistic skills.

Around A.D. 500, small-scale agriculture was introduced. Corn was grown to supplement hunting, fishing and gathering. It increased in importance until, by about A.D. 1000, it had become the main source of food.

The Niagarans of this period are known as the "Princess Point Culture." They tended to develop larger, more permanent camps on flood plains with small crops of corn planted in clearings. The mild climate of Niagara allowed a longer growing season, and, in addition to the corn, the forests and meadows, supplied many nuts, berries, herbs, vegetables and medicinal plants. The people's ability to hunt, fish, gather and grow more food enabled the land to support a larger population, and the number of people in Niagara grew accordingly. As the population grew, its system of government increased in complexity.

Towards A.D. 900 to A.D. 1000, at the time that the Vikings "discovered" America, people had lived in Niagara for nine or ten thousand years. By this time, agriculture had evolved to become of primary importance and this affected settlement patterns, giving rise to larger, more permanent villages. This marked the beginnings of the "Terminal Woodland" period, which lasted until contact with Europeans was made in the seventeenth century. It is also known as the period of the Ontario Iroquois tradition. Large populations, organized in complex societies with sophisticated trade and political relationships with other nations, are characteristic of this era.

This period was marked locally by extensive corn agriculture supplemented by fishing, hunting and gathering, supporting a large population living in well-situated villages and larger camps. The so-called "Glen Meyer Culture" built villages protected by sharpened wooden palisade walls, surrounded by large corn fields. These people developed into, or were gradually replaced by, the people of the "Pickering Culture" who similarly lived in large palisaded villages surrounded by fields of sunflowers, corn, beans and squash. The latter three crops became known to Iroquoian peoples as the "three sisters," grown together with the beans supported on the corn stalks as if they were stakes and the squash growing between rows. They became the most essential part of the Iroquoian diet.

The Water-fall of Niagara *(c. 1750) by Robert Hancock*

Tercentenary Celebration (1921) of Champlain's Landing in 1615, *attributed to Owen Staples*

the Niagara River from what is now Lewiston, New York, in 1626. Over the next fifty years, the area was seen by several more French explorers and the missionaries who accompanied them. Among the former was the famous Robert Cavalier de la Salle in 1669 and among the latter was Father Louis Hennepin, who was the first to publish an image of Niagara Falls. De la Salle wished to establish French control over the Great Lakes and the Mississippi valley to gain access to the riches of the interior of North America. His men built the first sailing ship, Le Griffon, somewhere above Niagara Falls and this became the first such ship to ply the waters of Lakes Erie and Huron.

The residents of the area at the time were an Iroquoian people known as the Neutral Nation. The first mention of the Neutrals was by Samuel de Champlain, who reported that Étienne Brûlé had visited some of their villages. The French referred to these people as "la Nation Neutre" because they traded with the Huron to the north of their territory and the Five Nations of Iroquois to the east and seemed to be at peace with both, a buffer between the warring Iroquois and

## The Coming of the French

The first European to visit this long-settled area was a French Franciscan friar, De la Roche Daillon, who crossed

*Re-enactment of life during the Late Iroquoian period*

Huron confederacies. At the time that the Neutral people were first encountered by the French there were as many as 40,000 Neutrals living in the area from present-day London through Brantford and Hamilton and throughout the Niagara Peninsula. They were a populous, powerful people but within several decades they were overcome by two "gifts" brought by the Europeans — firearms and diseases against which the First Nations had no immunity.

The Neutral people of Niagara, or the Onguiaronon as their neighbours called them, lived in large bark-covered longhouses in villages protected by walls formed by palisades of sharpened poles. Each longhouse was the dwelling for several families belonging to the same clan, related to each other by matrilineal descent. A man moved in with his wife's family, and their children would belong to the wife's clan. Each family group occupied an area of the longhouse and used shelves that lined the walls as sleeping platforms and as storage bins for their belongings. Several hearths running down the centre of the longhouse served the various families. They were smoky, crowded and undoubtedly noisy dwellings, but they served to keep kin close together and mutually supportive. This also meant that disease introduced to the longhouse would strike the entire household. Such dreaded European diseases as smallpox could wipe out 80 people in a longhouse within a few days.

Labour among the Neutral people was divided between the men and women along very well-established lines. While both sexes helped with the clearing of forests

*Re-enactment of Late Iroquoian village*

for planting crops, the women were the primary agriculturalists, planting the seed, hoeing the rows of crops, harvesting and storing and cooking the food. The men were toolmakers, hunters, fishermen and, whenever required, warriors. Women played an important role in the politics of the nation, and their voices were heard in the councils of village leaders.

The spiritual life of the Neutral was closely tied to their understanding of nature on which they depended for survival. Spirits inhabited woods and streams, the air, the water and the earth. Diseases and setbacks were caused by these spirits, and various ceremonies could be performed to appease them to cure disease, gain favour in the hunt or the harvest and generally help the people live more harmoniously in their surroundings. Many of these ceremonies — based on planting and harvesting, the seasons, birth, death and so on — ring familiar in the practices of most early cultures.

The balance of power was upset by the rapidly increasing arrivals of Europeans in the New World — English, French, Dutch and Spanish. Within a half century of the first encounters between the French and the Neutral, disease had reduced the numbers of Neutral people from as many as 40,000 to as few as 12,000. European political dealings with Native nations and the demand for European manufactured trade goods led to fierce struggles among Native people for control of trade networks. In the 1640s,

the powerful League of the Iroquois attacked and dispersed the Huron Nation around Georgian Bay. The Seneca Nation from what is now New York State invaded Neutral territory and was able to disperse or assimilate the Neutral people. By 1650, the Neutral villages were no more. The Senecas established small settlements in their new territory but did not stay. Chippewa traditions describe how the Chippewa, an Algonkian people, filled the vacuum created by the dispersal of the Neutrals and drove off the Seneca. By the end of the seventeenth century, Niagara was the sparsely populated hunting and fishing grounds of the Mississaugi-Chippewa Nation.

The Neutrals, once so populous in Niagara, left their dead, their artifacts and, most enduring of all, their name for the mighty river — Onguiaahra, a name that time has changed to Niagara. The meaning is lost to obscurity and has been translated as "the

*Effigy, Middle Iroquoian period*

thunderer" in reference to the Falls; more commonly it is translated as simply, but less poetically, "the strait."

\* \* \*

People have been active on the land surrounding Niagara-on-the-Lake for the last 10,000 years. Because of its rich past, the town requires developers to conduct archaeological surveys of their properties prior to construction if the building site is considered to be culturally sensitive. Every one of these recent projects has uncovered evidence of occupation going back thousands of years. Slowly the story of this ancient past is being unravelled.

# 3

# THE FIRST TOWN

More than a century elapsed between the time that the Niagara area was first explored by the French and its first settlement by Europeans. In the year 1726, the French built a strong fort on the east bank of the Niagara River at the point where it flows into Lake Ontario. The large stone building was constructed ostensibly for trade with the Natives but actually to maintain French sovereignty in the area. Fort Niagara played an

The Esplanade of Fort George, *1805, by Edward Walsh*

important role in the wars with the rival British for control of the continent throughout the first half of the century. It was finally captured by a British expedition in 1759.

British control of Fort Niagara would not last long. In 1775, the 13 American colonies rose up to throw off the bonds of British rule. The resulting American War of Independence dragged on for eight years, during which Niagara was an important British and American Loyalist base for operations against the rebellious colonies.

*French drummer, Fort Niagara, circa 1750*

The first white settlers on the site of Niagara-on-the-Lake were American refugees fleeing the excesses of the American Revolution in 1779. The town established here flourished and served briefly as the capital of the Province of Upper Canada (Ontario). But the refugees did not escape British-American rivalries. Niagara-on-the-Lake, known simply as Niagara, became a major battlefield during the War of 1812 and was captured, occupied and destroyed by an American army during that conflict.

## The Founding of the Town

In 1779 Fort Niagara became a haven for Loyalist refugees fleeing their rebel neighbours. Grief-stricken men, women and children, made homeless by the conflict in the American colonies, gathered at Niagara, dressed in rags and starving after trekking through the wilderness to reach safety. The refugees strained the food stores of the fort. In 1779, the British commander encouraged a few Loyalist families to cross to the west side of the river and plant crops

Fort Niagara from Fort George, *circa 1815, by J.H. Slade*

The American Revolution ended in 1783 with the 13 colonies gaining their independence as the United States of America. Some 50,000 Americans chose to remain loyal to King George and left the new country. Many of these United Empire Loyalists, along with a large number of Six Nations Native people, were given land in what is now Canada.

Butler's Rangers, a Loyalist regiment that had distinguished itself during the war, were settled on the land on which Niagara-on-the-Lake was built. In 1790 the government sent a plan for a town to be called "Lenox," but the settlement had already adopted the name Butlersburg after Lieutenant-Colonel John Butler. The name did not last. The place was finally surveyed in 1791 and became known by its ancient Neutral name, "Niagara."

in the vicinity of barracks built by Butler's Rangers the year before. In the next few years, more families joined them. This was the beginning of the charming town of Niagara-on-the-Lake.

War of Independence, the British refused to surrender the post to the Americans, pending settlement of other parts of the treaty with which the United States failed to comply. This included compensation for lands seized from the Loyalists. For the next 13 years the British maintained a garrison in American territory.

## The Provincial Capital

In the meantime, the village of Niagara continued to flourish. Its importance grew quickly. In 1791, Canada was divided into two provinces, Lower Canada, which became Quebec, and Upper Canada, now Ontario. That same year John Graves Simcoe, a British cavalry commander who had distinguished himself during the American Revolution, was appointed as the first Lieutenant-Governor of Upper Canada. He chose Niagara, conveniently located in the

"War Clouds," General John Graves Simcoe, First Governor of Upper Canada 1792 (1793), *after John David Kelly*

Although Fort Niagara was now in the territory of the new United States according to the treaty that ended the

centre of the new province (which still hugged the shores of Lakes Ontario and Erie) as the temporary capital.

Fort George from Old Niagara, *circa 1805, by Edward Walsh*

From the moment Simcoe and his wife Elizabeth arrived, Niagara-on-the-Lake took on the character of a cultured and cultivated place. While the Lieutenant-Governor established Government House at Navy Hall, converted a barracks building for the Houses of Parliament, and set about exploring the province and establishing laws, Elizabeth breathed life into the society of Niagara. Her diary describes the elegant dinners and balls she arranged. The officers of the military garrison, many of whom were from the upper crust of English society, offered the services of the military bands to play at dances and concerts, staged plays for the local public and brought refinement to what would otherwise have been a rough frontier outpost. This established a pattern for Niagara-on-the-Lake, still known for its culture and elegance.

Lieutenant-Governor Simcoe wanted to fast-track the new province's development. Progressive laws were introduced and there were grand engineering plans to build roads linking the new settlements. Names of towns were changed to give them an English flavour. Thus, Toronto became "York" and the town of Niagara became "Newark." One of the Native names by which the Mohawk referred to Simcoe, possibly out of his earshot, translates as "he who changes the names of everything."

Niagara-Newark was not to remain the capital for long. In 1796, by the terms of Jay's Treaty, Fort Niagara was handed over to an American garrison. This placed potentially hostile troops within gunshot of the capital. Simcoe ordered the construction of a new British fort in Newark — Fort George — and moved the capital to York. While many of Simcoe's innovations became the basis on which Ontario was built, other changes did not last. Within a couple of decades York reverted to its old Native name of Toronto. The ancient Neutral name of Niagara was revived by its inhabitants by 1798.

The town of Niagara continued to grow and was recognized as the main town of the Niagara region. Smart houses and thriving businesses were established. It was the centre for law, commerce and shipbuilding and was rapidly becoming an important agricultural centre with a growing tender fruit industry. Fort George was the headquarters of the British army in Southern Ontario and the main depot of the British Indian Department, which held large councils with the Native population on the Commons surrounding the fort. Niagara continued as the military and cultural hub of Southern Ontario.

# The War of 1812

From the 1790s until 1815, Britain was locked in a deadly struggle with revolutionary France. By the early 1800s, Napoleon Bonaparte threatened to conquer Europe and its colonies; the struggle turned into a world war fought on five continents. To prevent supplies reaching France, the British

*American infantry officer, 1812*

established an embargo preventing the United States and other neutral countries from trading with the French. Meanwhile, as American frontiersmen pushed west to take up new lands, wars broke out with the Native owners who were being displaced. The Americans accused the British of inciting and arming the Native nations.

These threats to American sovereignty could not last. On June 18, 1812, the United States declared war on Britain.

Canada would be the battleground. The Americans, whose population was ten times that of Upper Canada, realized that the British could spare few troops for the defence of Canada. Thomas Jefferson thought that taking Canada would be a "mere matter of marching." The matter of marching would turn into a bitter three-year struggle.

The United States had an army of regulars and militia that numbered in the tens of thousands, supported by a secure supply route through the states. The British in Ontario had only a small force of a few thousand regulars supported by militia and, they hoped, the support of the Native population. They also had a long and vulnerable supply route that followed the St. Lawrence-Great Lakes water system, the border with the United States. Their strength lay in their training. They had the most professional army in the world, while the American army was newly established and therefore among the most poorly trained.

News travelled slowly in the nineteenth century. When war was declared on June 18, the British in Washington quickly dispatched fast couriers to warn Britain's Upper Canadian posts of the declaration. The Americans sent word to their garrisons through their regular mail system. As a result, many of the American frontier commanders learned that their country had declared war from their British counterparts!

At Niagara, the officers of Fort George were entertaining the American officers of Fort Niagara at a mess dinner at Navy Hall when news of the

*Six Nations warrior, 1812*

war arrived. According to legend, the news that they were now at war caused a great commotion in the mess. The British officer in charge calmed the group, however, saying that there was no need to let bad news ruin a good dinner. The evening carried on and at the end the British escorted

The Battle of Queenston Heights, *attributed to James B. Dennis*

their American friends arm in arm to the dock whence the Americans were rowed back to their own fort. The war could now begin in earnest.

The man considered most responsible for the preservation of Upper Canada in the first year of the war, the most dangerous part of the war for the British, was General Isaac Brock, the commander of the British forces in Upper Canada in 1812 and the acting governor of the province. When war was declared, the local populace quickly assembled at Fort George to offer their services. Among the regiments of Lincoln County Militia mustered at the fort was a company composed of Canadians of African descent from the area. A body of warriors from the Six Nations reserve on the Grand River also arrived to help with the defence of the province.

Brock acted quickly, ordering the outnumbered garrison of Fort St. Joseph in the Sault Ste. Marie area to attack the American Fort Michilimackinac before the Americans in this isolated area were aware that war had been declared. In August he personally led an expedition to capture a larger American army at Detroit after which he hastily returned to his headquarters at Fort George to prepare for an expected American invasion of Niagara.

On October 13, 1812, an American army of 5,000 stationed in Lewiston started to cross the Niagara river to the small Upper Canadian village of Queenston. As the first thousand Americans landed on Canadian soil, they were met by a few hundred regulars and Canadian militia supported by a small band of Six Nations fighters. Brock

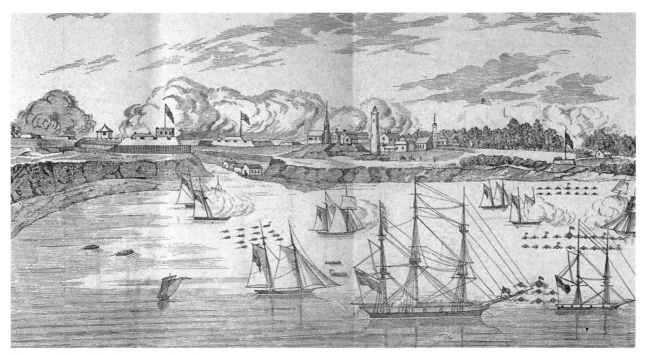

The Attack on Fort George, *artist unknown*

hastened to the scene after ordering all of his forces to march to join him at Queenston. On arrival, he took command of the small group already fighting at the village. The Americans had gained a strong position on the top of Queenston Heights. Brock organized his small force and led a bold attack up the heights, but was killed by an American rifleman.

Brock was dead, but his troops continued to be inspired by this forward-looking leader. As columns of reinforcements marched from Fort George and Chippawa, the Americans on the heights were kept hemmed in by bands of Native warriors, Canadian militia and British light infantry. The sight of the lines of feared red coats marching along the river road, their scarlet tunics standing out at a distance, proved too daunting to the poorly trained Americans waiting their turn to cross the Niagara River from Lewiston to reinforce their troops already on Canadian soil. Many refused to cross. As a result, within a few hours of Brock's death, some 1,300 American troops found themselves trapped on Queenston Heights by 1,100 British, Canadians and Natives. The British lined their men up in tight ranks,

two deep, fired a deafening volley from their muskets and charged with bayonets. The Americans panicked. Many fell to their deaths trying to rush down the escarpment, while others drowned trying to swim the swift Niagara to get back to the American shore. Most surrendered to the British. Thus, Niagara and perhaps Ontario were saved, but at a great cost. Brock was dead.

During the battle, the Americans in Fort Niagara had not been idle. They fired cannons at Fort George, setting several buildings on fire — including the powder magazine. There was enough gunpowder in the magazine to destroy the fort if the fire reached it. Racing against time, a few volunteers quelled the flames before they could reach the powder, and the fort was saved.

*Officer,*
*Lincoln Militia, 1812*

Following the Battle of Queenston Heights, a short truce was negotiated on the Niagara frontier. Brock and his mortally wounded aide-de-camp John Macdonnell were buried in a state funeral in one of the bastions of Fort George. During the funeral, the gallant American commander at Fort Niagara had his cannons fire a salute to honour the hero Brock. War was still considered to be a civilized affair.

The Americans remained quiet during the winter but continued to reinforce the area. On April 27, 1813, they struck again, launching an amphibious operation against York (Toronto), which they captured after the destruction of Fort York. They did not occupy the capital, but burned government buildings and carried off government supplies before returning to Fort Niagara.

On May 25, the American fleet in the mouth of the Niagara River, supported by the guns of Fort Niagara, opened up a massive bombardment of the greatly outgunned Fort George. Red-hot cannonballs and exploding shells soon set the fort's wooden buildings on fire. Within a few hours every building in the fort and at Navy Hall was consumed — except for the stone powder magazine. It still survives as the oldest building in Niagara-on-the-Lake.

Two days later, British outposts guarding the shores of Lake Ontario gazed out over the fog-shrouded lake to see a frightening sight. Several thousand Americans were rowing ashore, protected by the guns of the American fleet. The small British force of regulars, Canadian militia and Native warriors, outnumbered ten to one by the invasion force, fought to stem the tide but suffered heavy casualties. The battle advanced from the lakeshore through the town, and finally the British force was driven out. The Americans had captured Niagara and the ruins of Fort George. This time they were determined to stay.

The American army occupied the town and reinforced Fort George, strengthening its defences. Their intention was to use the fort as a bridgehead from which the invasion of Canada could be launched. Defeats of American armies at the Battle of Stoney Creek on June 6 and the Battle of Beaver Dams a few weeks later forced a change of plans.

Fort George did not prove a secure base. Throughout the summer and autumn of 1813, the Americans were kept locked up in the fort, unable to exploit their bridgehead to invade the rest of the province. Their sentries were continually attacked and patrols ambushed in the forests. Meanwhile, the British continued to gain reinforcements and by late autumn were prepared to recapture the position.

The American garrison of Fort George was greatly reduced, deployed elsewhere for other campaigns, and many of the men who remained became ill. At the end of the year, when their terms of enlistment ended, a large number of militia prepared to return to the States. Meanwhile, the British army was advancing towards Fort George. The Americans had no choice but to abandon the fort and town and return to Fort Niagara in Youngstown, New York. On their retreat, on December 10, 1813, they committed what was then considered to be a great atrocity — they burned the entire town of Niagara prior to their departure, supposedly to deprive the British of winter quarters. Ironically, most of the burning was done by the "Canadian Volunteers," a regiment of disaffected Canadians in the service of the United States.

The British arrived at Niagara on the tail of the American retreat and immediately took steps to help the dispossessed civilians. Nine days later, revenge was taken. The British quietly crossed the Niagara River at night and stormed Fort Niagara, capturing it at bayonet point. Soon parties of Canadian militia, Natives and British regulars took revenge for the burning of Niagara and set torch to American communities from Fort Niagara to Buffalo. The War of 1812 had become total war.

Powder Magazine, Fort George, built 1794, Niagara-on-the-Lake, Canada.

*Powder magazine, Fort George, before restoration in 1936*

Battle of Lundy's Lane, *artist unknown*

In 1814, a better trained American army made a last attempt to capture Canada. On July 3, they invaded and took Fort Erie. Marching down the Niagara River they met and defeated a British army at the Battle of Chippawa and continued their advance until they surrounded the town of Niagara where they were supposed to rendezvous with the American fleet and retake the town. The fleet never arrived, however, and the American force retreated back up the river, now followed by a British force. The two armies met at Lundy's Lane in what is now Niagara Falls, Ontario, and here, the fiercest battle of the war in Canada was fought to a stalemate.

The Americans continued to retire, taking up a position in Fort Erie around which the British laid siege. After some failed attacks and bloody losses, the British failed to capture Fort Erie and retreated from the scene in mid-autumn. The Americans decided to abandon Canadian soil for the winter, blew up Fort Erie and crossed back to the American side to re-equip for the 1815 campaign. It was not to be, however. On Christmas Eve, 1814, the Treaty of Ghent was signed to end the war.

***

Niagara had been born of war, settled by those fleeing the American Revolution in the 1770s. It had only been settled for a few decades when war struck again. The War of 1812 was devastating for the town. Virtually all its homes, businesses and churches were turned to piles of ashes. Fruit trees were cut down, belongings looted or destroyed, livestock driven off and the people left with nothing. However, the people of Niagara were made of stern stuff. Returning to the ruins of their village, they began to rebuild, and like a phoenix, Niagara rose again from the ashes.

# 4

# NIAGARA REBORN

Following the War of 1812, the people of Niagara rebuilt their town. Once again it was established as the administrative centre of the district with courts, a jail and lawyers' offices. The importance of its location at one end of the portage route around Niagara Falls meant that the merchants in town flourished. But the development of the second Welland Canal in the 1840s severely threatened the town's transhipping and warehousing businesses and, within two decades, the town was locked in a severe economic depression. The early nineteenth century, like other periods in the town's past, was marked by incredible booms and devastating busts.

## Rebuilding the Town

On the British reoccupation of Niagara, Fort George and the town were little more than heaps of ashes. The British army reoccupied Fort George while adding two new military installations, Fort Mississauga and Butler's Barracks. Lessons had been learned during the war. Fort George

*St. Mark's Rectory, 17 Byron Street*

*69 Prideaux Street*

*St. Mark's Church*

had proven to be poorly located, too far from the mouth of the river to guard its entrance and yet too close to American gun batteries to be useful as a supply depot. Thus, Butler's Barracks, the new depot, was located some distance from American cannon positions while Fort Mississauga was a strong, compact citadel built at the river mouth. Because American shelling during the conflict had hit a number of buildings in the town, the decision was also made to move the town further inland.

This resulted in the expansion of the town's boundaries. Government buildings were to be located further west and citizens were encouraged to rebuild farther from the river. An area south of John Street and east of King Street was donated for the purpose by William Dickson. The land surrounding Fort Mississauga was privately owned by James Crooks, a merchant and land speculator. To keep the fields of fire from the fort clear of buildings, the government granted a little over 21 acres of land south and east of King Street to Crooks in exchange for his land surrounding Fort Mississauga in 1822. All of this expanded "New Survey" land was available to Niagarans who were rebuilding the town. Those who had lost their houses and outbuildings during the destruction of the town were able to submit "War Losses Claims" to the government, which gave them the capital to begin rebuilding.

In spite of the suggestion that the townsfolk build their new homes and businesses farther from the river, Niagarans proved to be (and still are) a rather conservative and feisty

lot. Most rebuilt on the ruins of their former houses. Merchants rebuilt on Prideaux and Queen Streets, and residents constructed new houses in the original town plot, some recycling the foundations and cellars of their earlier houses. The Anglicans were able to salvage a good portion of St. Mark's Church, while the Presbyterians rebuilt on the lot where their first church had been destroyed.

Niagara was once again the district seat, the centre for law and administration for Lincoln, Dundas and Wentworth counties, and a new courthouse and jail were built to serve the region. Following military recommendations, they were located within the new town limits, well out of range of future American gunfire. The caution of the government proved groundless or the optimism of the townsfolk proved prophetic, for the town was never again threatened by American artillery or invasion.

## A Social and Commercial Centre

Within a decade, the town was again flourishing with neat streets of houses and commercial buildings. Niagara society reestablished itself and the British garrison supplied the musicians for town concerts and balls while the officers occasionally entertained the gentry with plays and other diversions.

Niagara again became an important forwarding point for the shipping of goods into the interior of the rapidly growing province. Manufactured goods, wines and spices from Europe, India and China came by ship to Niagara and were sent up the portage road beyond the falls by wagon for shipment west, while Canadian goods such as whisky, grain, fish and furs were shipped the opposite way. Because of its location on the portage route and its role as centre for the district, it was the destination for people with mercantile or legal business. As a result, Niagara boasted a large number of inns, taverns and hotels. At these establishments the traveller was able to buy a meal or a drink of ale or fine imported wine, to rent a sleeping room or a mattress in a large common sleeping room, or even gamble in one of many gaming rooms.

With the end of the Napoleonic Wars and the new peaceful relations with the United States, not only commerce and immigration but also tourism increased at a remarkable pace. Niagara Falls, a wonder of the world, was a "must see" for any worldly European lady or

Niagara Falls from the Canadian Side, *attributed to Hippolite Victor Valentin Sebron*

gentleman and the town of Niagara was a natural stopover during this journey into the wilds of Canada. As the 1820s progressed, more frequent schooner trips from Toronto and Kingston carried tourists to Niagara who then travelled to the falls by stage coach. Hotels, taverns, oyster bars and restaurants continued to spring up in Niagara to serve the travelling public. Soon steamboats replaced the sailing ships as excursion boats and as haulers of freight to Niagara and to Queenston. A few merchants grew extremely wealthy from the business of transhipping goods from Niagara into the interior of the country.

*The Whale Inn*

## The Age of Steam

In 1832, the Niagara Harbour and Dock Company established docks and shipbuilding facilities on the river to capitalize on the increasing trade across Lake Ontario and the important position of Niagara as a forwarding depot. For a few years, the company was a huge success, constructing a number of large steamers for the lake trade. At its

St. Andrew's Presbyterian Church, Niagara-on-the-Lake (Ontario), *1911, by Owen Staples*

height it employed over 400 men at good wages. One of their finest craft was a side-wheeled, ice-breaking steamship — the "Chief Justice Robinson."

The increasing numbers of workers, sailors and visitors to the town saw a further increase in the number of inns. Two of them survive, the Whale Inn as a private residence and the Moffatt Inn, which continues to cater to guests. To help the people manage the new wealth, two banks were established in town and of course more businesses opened on Queen Street. The dock company continued to add wharves, warehouses, a foundry and other facilities. Blacksmith shops, livery stables and other service industries grew apace.

Among the many engineers and technicians attracted by the company were a number of Scots Presbyterians, and it was at this time that the beautiful Presbyterian church was rebuilt on the spot where the earlier church had stood. Some of Niagara's growing African-Canadian population joined Reverend John Oakley's Baptist congregation. Gradually, the congregation became primarily African-Canadian. The increasing Irish population, particularly those who arrived following the Potato Famine of the 1840s, swelled the ranks of Niagara's Roman Catholic population, and St. Vincent de Paul Church, begun in 1834, was enlarged.

William Lyon Mackenzie *by John Wycliffe Lowes Forster*

## Rebellion

Newly prosperous Niagara was not always peaceful, however. Politics came to play an increasing role in the lives of the inhabitants. The rule of the old Loyalist "Family Compact," which controlled much of the government, was challenged with serious consequences. Following the War of 1812, a political gadfly named Robert Gourlay wrote newspaper articles and eventually a book highly critical of the government and the ruling elite. He was charged with sedition, tried at the Niagara Court House and eventually banished from the province. In 1824 a young Scots firebrand named William Lyon Mackenzie arrived in Niagara and set up a newspaper, *The Colonial Advocate*, in Queenston. Mackenzie's criticism of government became increasingly radical as the years passed. Gourlay and Mackenzie reflected the viewpoint of many Canadians. Complaints against the government were heard throughout the province and the time seemed ripe for change, by force of arms if necessary. By 1837, Mackenzie, now in Toronto, led a rebellion against the government that led to the occupation of Navy Island above Niagara Falls and a series of invasions of Canada by armed rebels and American sympathizers. Ultimately, the rebellion was put down by British regulars and the loyal Canadian militia.

While the radical movement tended to polarize the populace, the Niagara men remained primarily loyal and quickly formed themselves into militia companies to help quell the rebellion. A group of Niagara firemen, on learning of the outbreak of the rebellion in Toronto, commandeered a steamer and immediately sailed to the capital to aid in its defence. Once again, many of the inhabitants of African descent formed their own militia company to fight for the crown and remained incorporated for several years to help guard the Welland Canal. Fort Mississauga, lightly garrisoned prior to the rebellion, was reinforced, and the Niagara men stood on guard awaiting an attack that never came.

A final act of the rebellion occurred on April 17, 1840. Benjamin Lett, an exiled Irish-Canadian rebel, who was also a member of the nationalistic Young Ireland movement, planted a gunpowder charge in Brock's Monument, the tomb and memorial raised to the famous "Hero of Upper Canada" in 1824. The resulting explosion cracked the monument and broke the hearts of loyal Canadians who were outraged by this act of vandalism. Lett, who had a longstanding grievance against the militia and the British army, got his revenge. By 1854, however, enough money was raised to build a new Brock's Monument, which still stands guard over Queenston Heights.

Following the collapse of the rebellion in 1838, many of the captured rebels were housed in Niagara's jail before

*Brock's Monument, Queenston Heights*

being sentenced to execution or banishment to Australia. The old jail was witness to many dramatic scenes at that time. Not only was it the place of incarceration of rebels and felons, but it was also used as a debtors' prison. Several pathetic stories of the plight of these debtors survive.

Other stories surrounding the jail make us wonder at the cold-bloodedness of the times. In October 1826, two men charged with horse stealing and sheep stealing were to be publicly hanged at the jail. The event drew thousands to the area, particularly from the United States. To the great disappointment of the crowd, the men were reprieved and the executions did not take place. One entrepreneur even tried to sue the government for not carrying out the sentences. He had brought in a wagonload of gingerbread and cakes to be sold to the audience and was forced to let them go at a reduced rate, losing his money on the enterprise.

*Miss Rye's home for girls, circa 1901*

Another scene that occurred at the jail involved the fate of an African American named Moseby, who had escaped slavery in Kentucky and had fled to Canada. In escaping, he had stolen the slave master's horse. In 1837, the Canadian government was pressured to extradite the fugitive to face "justice" in the States. Moseby was locked in the Niagara jail. On the day he was to be shipped to the States, a contingent of citizens of African descent gathered at the jail to block his transport. In the confusion, two protesters were killed and Moseby escaped, apparently with some help from his jailor. This incident caused a great deal of public indignation and forced the Canadian government to rethink its response to the fugitive slave laws of the United States. A ruling was made that Canada would only extradite people who had committed crimes that would be considered felonies under Canadian law and because the government did not recognize slavery, they would not return those who had escaped from that abomination.

Since the arrival of the Loyalists, Niagara had always had a small population of people of African descent who blended into Niagara society. In the mid-nineteenth century, the town became a refuge for people escaping slavery, travelling through the network known as the "Underground Railroad." Some of these freedom seekers settled here and added to the prosperity of the town.

The jailhouse, courthouse, execution yard and perhaps the prison burying ground where these many dramas unfolded no longer exist. After they ceased to be used for their original purpose they were converted into "Our Western Home," opened in 1869 by Miss Rye. Impoverished girls from England were brought here to be trained in domestic skills and find jobs as servants in area homes. The institution was eventually closed in 1913 and the buildings were demolished. Today, the area is a park where children play their summer games, unaware of the stories that took place on that soil. Rumours of ghostly sightings in the park may be all that is left from that era.

## Economic Downturn

In 1824 several businessmen with vision began to build the Welland Canal to link Lake Ontario with Lake Erie, thereby bypassing Niagara Falls and ending the need for a portage route. This would eventually mean trouble for business in Niagara. The first canal, however, which opened in 1829, could handle only small vessels and was not a threat to Niagara's transhipping business. By 1836, this first Welland Canal was in trouble, suffering from a lack of maintenance capital. The government finally took over this hitherto private enterprise and began a second canal in 1841, replacing the wooden locks with stone-lined locks served by new wooden lock gates. Work continued throughout the 1840s.

The second Welland Canal enlarged the first, allowing larger steamers to move between the lakes. At the same time, beginning in 1846, Britain was repealing the Corn Laws, which provided Canadian farmers with preferential trade agreements with the empire. This helped bring on an economic depression. These circumstances effectively killed the business of "forwarding" or transhipping goods over the Niagara portage. Fewer ships landed their goods at Niagara and the lucrative bubble of the Niagara Dock Company was burst. As its debt load increased, the business started to shut down. The last steamer was built in Niagara in 1847.

In 1853, railway baron Samuel Zimmerman purchased the defunct Niagara Dock Company lands, and things looked promising for another economic boom in town. Zimmerman extended the Erie and Ontario Railway through town to the dock and constructed a railway car factory here. The enterprise soon ended, however, after Zimmerman was killed in the Desjardins Canal Disaster when the train in which he was riding broke through a bridge and plummeted into the canal. While the railway line into Niagara remained open, the carriage factory closed by 1861. Without Zimmerman's entrepreneurial know-how, the venture failed.

The Welland Canal had brought prosperity to its terminus on Lake Ontario. The town of Shipman's Corners, now known as St. Catharines, grew as manufacturers and their workers located along the canal. By the late 1840s, the old district that incorporated the Niagara Peninsula along with Hamilton and Wentworth, and of which Niagara was the district centre, was dismantled. Government and the court system were to be arranged on a township and county basis. Talk was that the county seat would be moved from Niagara to the rapidly growing centre of St. Catharines. In response, Niagara undertook the construction of a new county courthouse on Queen Street in Niagara in the hopes that the town would remain a judicial centre and therefore continue its other important roles as county centre. The solid stone building, completed in 1847, was not enough to stave off the inroads being made by St. Catharines. The county seat was established at St. Catharines in 1862.

\* \* \*

The first few decades following the War of 1812 saw the rapid rebuilding of the town and an economic surge, followed by an economic depression — both related to transportation. Niagara's location at one end of the portage route around Niagara Falls was responsible for the boom. The economic downturn began when the Welland Canal effectively allowed ships to move between Lakes Ontario and Erie, thus ending the portaging or forwarding trade. The loss of business to the Welland Canal, the demise of the dock company, the closing of the railroad coach factory and the loss of prestige that came when the county seat was moved created a severe economic depression. Hotels, taverns, restaurants and businesses closed, people went bankrupt and a cloud hung over Niagara.

It is hard to keep a good town down, however. Niagara would rise again.

*Welland Canal today*

# 5

# THE FIRST WAVE OF TOURISM

*Queen St., circa 1907*

The years between 1860 and 1945 saw great highs as well as lows for Niagara. Although the town had slipped into an economic depression by the early 1860s, the stimulation of trade during the American Civil War helped create new wealth by mid-decade. By the 1870s a very healthy tourism industry had developed, and Niagara entered a golden age. Wealthy Canadians and Americans flocked to the town to stay in its luxurious hotels and, in many cases, to build their own palatial summer homes. This long period of success lasted until the advent

Cayuga, *circa 1905*

of the automobile made day trips feasible and the Great Depression sounded the death knell of the economy. By the end of World War II, the outlook for the town was once again bleak.

## Civil War and Fenian Troubles

The American Civil War that tore the United States apart between 1861 and 1865 brought business to the resourceful people of Niagara. The Reciprocity Treaty of 1854 had allowed the free passage of Canadian goods across the border. The American appetite was insatiable. Fortunes were made shipping agricultural goods and manufactured items to the embattled States.

At the same time, Niagara became a centre of intrigue frequented by Confederate spies and saboteurs. Several plots were hatched by these rebel commandos in 1863 to seize U.S. shipping on Lake Erie, to free Confederate

Battle of Ridgeway, *artist unknown*

prisoners of war from Northern prisons and to generally create havoc behind the lines, launching raids from Canadian soil. While locally, these schemes amounted to nothing, a successful raid had been launched from Quebec against banks in St. Albans, Vermont, in October 1864. The raiders were seized by Canadian authorities but the Canadian public lionized these daring Southern "heroes." Eventually, the British-Canadian courts freed the rebels. This infuriated the government of the United States and war almost broke out over this and other disputes. The British responded by increasing the number of troops at vulnerable points and calling out the militia to discourage Confederate raids and to prepare to defend Canada against possible United States action. At Niagara, Fort Mississauga was again garrisoned and the troops of Butler's Barracks put on alert.

Immediately following the Civil War, the peace of the Niagara region was shattered by an unexpected invasion. Thousands of veterans of the Northern army were discharged, but a lack of jobs following the war meant that many of these men, particularly those from the cities, were unable to find work. A large number were first- or second-generation Irish-Americans who harboured grievances against England. They formed an American "Fenian Brotherhood" to fight for Irish independence, and while some travelled to the Emerald Isle to join rebels in the homeland, others hatched an intriguing scheme. The Fenians planned to invade Canada, recruit from the large population of Irish-Canadians and capture what is now Ontario and Quebec, then known as Canada West and Canada East. The invaders would then trade Canada back to Britain in return for Ireland's independence.

In 1866 the Fenians invaded from Buffalo and landed at Fort Erie. Their intention was to capture the major rail lines and with reinforcements travel to the major centres to cut communications and easily conquer the province. They defeated a Canadian militia force at the Battle of Ridgeway fought near Fort Erie, but learned that expected Irish-Canadian support would not be forthcoming and that the American government was preventing more American Fenians from reinforcing the invaders. The invasion ended rather abruptly and the invaders were arrested by American authorities as they tried to retreat back to the Buffalo area. Peace returned to Niagara, and its entrepreneurs could concentrate on business.

## The Queen's Royal Hotel

The ratepayers of Lincoln County voted to establish the county seat and the county court in St. Catharines in 1862. With the removal of the court to St. Catharines, the town fathers of Niagara sought compensation from the provincial government for the resulting financial losses to the town. The courthouse, built at a high cost in 1847, became the Town Hall with the incorporation of Niagara, but it was too grandiose a building for that purpose. It was more than the town could afford now that its costs would not be offset by the grants available to a provincial court. Again, influential Niagarans petitioned the government for funds to pay the $8,000 still owed for the building to alleviate the burden on the taxpayers.

The province eventually agreed that Niagara should be compensated, and the county was ordered to pay the $8,000. The town leaders showed their innovation and willingness to take risks by using the money to invest rather than immediately paying their debt. They planned on paying the outstanding balance on the courthouse over time through higher taxes, while the town partnered with the private sector and used the $8,000 for the construction of a magnificent hotel situated on the banks of the river. The hotel, initially called the Royal Niagara and eventually known as the Queen's Royal, was the catalyst that began a new age of prosperity for the town.

The Queen's Royal Hotel set a standard for elegance at its opening in 1866. The beautiful four-storey white struc-

ture, set on the rivershore, featured excellent service, uniformed bellhops, fine dining, and scenic vistas from its airy balconies and veranda. The hotel had a beautiful green for lawn bowling, a major share in the new golf course constructed at Fort Mississauga, and tennis courts that were of such quality that the Championship of Canada was played there in 1907. Its greatest glory came in 1901 when the Duke of York (later King George V) and the Duchess (later Queen Mary) stayed at the hotel for a few days. Niagara could now accommodate the most discerning guests in world-class style — a tradition continued by the fine hotels of Niagara-on-the-Lake today.

The American Civil War had stimulated business in Niagara and also brought great prosperity to American industrialists who had supplied the war machine at inflated prices. With the end of the war, many of these wealthy Americans began to travel, not only to Europe but to Canada. The elegant Queen's Royal Hotel, well marketed to the wealthy on both sides of the border, attracted a slate of influential customers. Many of these visitors fell in love with the beautiful town and its setting, its tranquil tree-lined streets and its excellent hotels and restaurants, not to mention the relatively mild climate. The town's proximity to the ever-popular Niagara Falls was also a key to its growing popularity. As the century progressed, several of these wealthy visitors constructed huge, elaborate summer homes in Niagara as refuges from their busy schedules.

*Queen's Royal Hotel, circa 1910*

*Tennis, circa 1910*

## Steamboats and the Railway

With the beginnings of this tourism, regular steamers began to arrive from Toronto. Captain Milloy, whose large home became the Oban Inn, started a steamship service from Toronto to Niagara, while the Niagara Navigation Company was created in 1878 to offer regular trips from Toronto to Lewiston and Queenston. Within a few years this company purchased the Niagara dock from Milloy's estate and operated several elegant steamers: the *Chicora*, the *Chippawa*, the *Corona*, the *Cibola* and later the *Cayuga* on the Toronto-to-Niagara run. Prior to 1910, the steamers each made six daily trips between city and town and attracted wealthy and not-so-wealthy tourists. The steamers offered elegant rooms and facilities as well as holds for shipping Niagara fruit to the Toronto markets. By 1914, the Niagara Navigation Company

*Queen Street, circa 1930*

was bought out by Canada Steamship Lines, which continued to operate at least one of the steamers, the *Cayuga*, until 1957. The ship sailed for another two years under new owners and then finally was scrapped in 1959. A long-standing superstition against giving ships names ending in the letter "a" was proven unfounded by the longevity of the Niagara steamers.

A railway from Chippawa to Niagara — the Michigan Central Railway — made travel from Buffalo, itself linked to all of the major centres by rail, an easy and comfortable undertaking. In the summer of 1910, five trains ran daily to Buffalo. In 1914, an electric railway was built, with trains arriving from St. Catharines hourly during the day. Soon the rail and water traffic boomed and large numbers of visitors came for a day, a weekend or a season. Service industries sprang up and again a residential building boom began with the new-found wealth brought by tourism.

Tourists stayed in the Queen's Royal, the refurbished Moffat Inn, Prince of Wales or one of the town's several other small inns and guest houses. Many stayed with friends who had built large summer homes in the town. They entertained themselves with excursions to Niagara Falls and by boating on the river, swimming in the lake, lawn bowling, golfing, playing tennis or croquet and visiting Niagara's historic sites.

*The Golf Club, circa 1910*

## Cultural Movements

While Niagara's merchants and service industries developed, the town's cultural side, present since the days of Simcoe, similarly flourished. In the 1880s, a cultural, semi-religious but non-sectarian phenomenon known as the "Chautauqua movement" was established in Chautauqua County, New York. The movement was really a summer gathering of people to listen to poetry, paint, participate in debate, attend theatre and, in general, pursue wholesome cultural activities. Prominent Torontonians moved to establish a Canadian Chautauqua in Niagara and purchased a 92-acre plot of land on the north end of Niagara. In 1887, this "Niagara Assembly" of the Chautauqua movement erected a tent city and attracted hundreds of people who came together for worship, poetry recitations, study and contemplation.

*Chautauqua Hotel, circa 1900*

Within four years, the Chautauqua grounds boasted a 4,000-seat amphitheatre, a large three-storey hotel and numerous cottages occupied by summer patrons. A rail spur connected the camp with the main line. Educational programs, lectures, concerts and seminars stimulated patrons from among the elite of nearby Canadian and American cities. These were people ahead of their time. In 1891, lectures dealt with "the woman question," exploring the role of women in current and future society. The movement focused not only on the mind and the soul but also on the body. Numerous recreational facilities were offered by the Chautauqua hotel — lawn bowling, tennis, croquet, baseball, swimming and boating.

The Niagara Assembly never really became financially strong and in 1894 faced foreclosure on the camp. A new company, the Niagara Syndicate, took over and struggled on for the next decade and a half. In 1909, however, the hotel burned. The property was sold in 1910 and again in 1918. Within a few years the Mississauga Beach Land Company, the new owners, subdivided the land and sold off the building lots. Today, the Chautauqua neighbourhood is a charming and unique part of Niagara-on-the-Lake with small lots and many former cottages renovated as permanent residences.

The Niagara Historical Society was established in this period. In the 1880s, the centennial of the town and the province stirred a growing interest in the town's history. As the twentieth century approached, the need to preserve history became a driving force for some and in 1896, Janet Carnochan, a retired teacher, met with fourteen other residents and founded the society as an important cultural resource.

The Historical Society began a program of collecting and publishing documents related to local history. They also collected local artifacts at a time when museums usually

*Troops at Camp Niagara, circa 1914*

collected only foreign curiosities. The society erected a num-ber of stone markers in the area to commemorate impor-tant people and events and was instrumental in ensuring that the government preserved the site of Fort George and the old building remaining from Navy Hall.

By 1907, Carnochan had been able to beg, borrow and raise enough money to build a museum for the society's col-lection. Memorial Hall, the oldest structure in Ontario built as a museum still stands, housing an important collection of local artifacts — from a chair used in the first meeting of Simcoe's parliament to Isaac Brock's hat. In 1949, the museum was expanded when the adjacent high school building was acquired. The complex was largely restored in 1997-98, andupgrading still continues.

*Memorial Hall, 1911*

*Troops at Camp Niagara, circa 1914*

## Camp Niagara

At the same time, the mili-tary's long role in Niagara was changing. Since the time of Simcoe, regular army garrisons of varying sizes had

*Camp Niagara, circa 1918*

manned first Fort George and then Fort Mississauga and Butler's Barracks. The prospects of peace following the Civil War (upset briefly by the Fenian Raids) and the for-mation of the new Dominion of Canada in 1867, com-bined with an austerity program in Britain, led the British to force Canada to develop its own defences. The old forts of Niagara were turned over to Canada. By 1870, the British troops were withdrawn.

To set up its own defence system, Canada reformed the Militia Act and provided for serious training of its citizen soldiers. Butler's Barracks and the Commons at Niagara

became Camp Niagara, a massive summer militia training camp that made its own impact on the town. Providing groceries and entertainment facilities for the thousands of troops who lived in tents on the Commons during the summer made many an entrepreneur's fortune. The militia also became a focus for the social life in the town, performing Sunday band concerts and taking part in parades, sports days and other activities. A golf club, one of the first built in North America, and a race course were created largely through the efforts of militia officers. The first movie theatre was established and vaudeville pro-ductions were presented in the courthouse primarily to entertain the troops.

## World Wars and Depression

In 1914, Canada became involved in World War I. Young men enlisted to fight for their country, serving in various army battalions or in the navy. Camp Niagara became a serious place as it trained young men for the horrors of trench warfare. The Commons and the golf course at Fort

*The War Memorial Clock Tower, circa 1930*

impact on local stores, taverns and places of entertainment and on the social life of the town. The sacrifice of Niagara's military men was not forgotten, however. In 1922, the Clock Tower was designed by Charles Wilmot and erected on Queen Street as a war memorial to the Niagara men who died in the Great War. Even the erection of this lasting monument, now such an important part of the downtown streetscape, was debated by those who just wanted to forget the war.

By the 1920s, the popularity of the automobile put a gradual end to the elegant lake steamers that once ran a regular daily service between Niagara-on-the-Lake and Toronto. More travellers opted to drive rather than take public transit. In 1929, the heaviest blow fell with the onset of the Great Depression. The Depression killed the economy of Niagara. The electic railway ceased operation in 1931. Businesses closed down, tourism slowed to a trickle, hotels went bankrupt and many of the great houses were abandoned by their once-wealthy owners.

The Queen's Royal Hotel itself had been in financial difficulties as early as 1920, struggling with the age of the automobile, a short tourist season and increasing maintenance costs. It went bankrupt and was sold in 1925. The new owners first sold off its land, then its furniture and parts of the building, which was finally demolished in 1931.

Mississauga were torn up as troops dug practice trenches. Travel restrictions and food rationing killed the tourism trade, and while the town was not economically depressed, its mood had changed.

Among the odder and least-known pages of the town's history at the time of the war was the Polish army's presence at Camp Niagara. In late 1917, the Allies formed a Polish government in exile, headed by the Polish patriot, pianist and composer Ignace Paderewski. A Polish army was recruited in the United States from young men of Polish descent, paid for by France and trained in Canada. Thousands of young Polish Americans arrived in town. Hundreds of these young men lie buried on the battlefields of France and Belgium. Others who fell prey to disease, accident and the great influenza epidemic at the end of the war stayed in Niagara-on-the-Lake, buried in a special section of the Catholic cemetery. Each year in June a memorial service is held on "Polish Sunday" to remember these young men.

When the war ended in 1918, the veterans returned home. Ten Niagarans had died in the conflict. Tourism gradually returned to Niagara but the military presence diminished. A tide of anti-militarism and pacifism combined with government cash shortages forced a reduction in the summer militia camps. This in turn had a negative

*Queen Street, circa 1940*

*Powder magazine, Fort George*

\* \* \*

During the 1930s people struggled just to survive. In a move to regenerate tourism, create jobs and instill pride, the government undertook a series of public works during this period. The Queen Elizabeth Way was built to encourage tourism to Niagara and plans were made to reconstruct Fort George, which had been burned during the War of 1812. Only the intrepid 1796 powder magazine, which had survived everything that the enemy and time could do to destroy it, and the earthworks remained of the fort. As a Depression make-work project, gangs of men were hired to rebuild the old fort. Construction was completed by 1940, but another war delayed its opening for five years.

World War II would take another generation of Niagarans off to war in this great struggle for democracy, and another 18 would pay the ultimate sacrifice. During the war, Niagara-on-the-Lake continued on in the same way as other small towns in Ontario. The town had become somewhat of a backwater, rich in history and location but economically unimportant.

The eight decades between 1862 and World War II had been a period of boom and bust. The end of the nineteenth century saw the rapid growth of tourism as the wealthy travelled to the beautiful little town to stay in luxury hotels, and enjoy the mild climate and fine location. Steamship and rail service grew rapidly to serve these travellers.

The town had also taken a new name for itself. In the waning years of the nineteenth century, with the Canadian town at the falls naming itself Niagara Falls, there were frequent mix-ups in mail delivery. Niagara was renamed Niagara-on-the-Lake, to end the confusion. One historian described this as the town's most beautiful name of all.

The advent of the automobile heralded the beginning of the day-trip and the end of the great age of rail travel. Gradually, hotels in Niagara went bankrupt and transportation services were cut back. The town's weakened economy was delivered a final blow by the Great Depression. By the end of World War II, the impoverished town was heading towards obscurity.

# 6

# NIAGARA RESTORED

*20 Platoff Street*

buildings. Their work was noticed, and more citizens and visitors caught the restoration fever. By the 1970s, restoration in Niagara was a way of life and property values soared. While all this went on, another group of Niagarans was creating the Shaw Festival and nurturing it through its early years to establish it as a successful annual event. This combination of heritage preservation and cultural development has been the key to the town's present-day popularity.

At the end of World War II, Niagara-on-the-Lake had few jobs and little industry, and presented limited prospects. It had its history and its tattered old buildings, some of which had stood for over 130 years but little else. Fortunately, a small group of citizens recognized the value of the town's history. While cities and towns elsewhere in Canada tore down the old to build the new, Niagara residents began restoring their old homes and

## Postwar Construction

In the decade following the end of World War II, much of the rest of Ontario experienced a renaissance. The current generation, a product of the Great Depression, made worldly by their war experiences, wanted change. Postwar prosperity brought jobs, and the deprivations of six years of war brought a boom in marriages and childbirths. Young couples, with jobs and disposable income, were able to buy homes through government-guaranteed mortgages, had their eyes firmly fixed on the future, and tended to reject the past. All over Ontario, century-old oak furniture inherited from parents was discarded for futuristic Arborite, aluminum and plastic. Old houses were thoroughly renovated with smart aluminum windows or were demolished to make room for bungalows and split levels with garages for the family automobile. Towns were stripped of heritage structures, which were replaced by boxy modern designs. The age of housing subdivisions and bedroom communities was launched with a vengeance.

*55 Prideaux Street*

Many young men and women returned to Niagara-on-the-Lake only to eventually move out again, closer to where the jobs were — in St. Catharines, Niagara Falls, Hamilton and Toronto. They helped to fill the new subdivisions, which were in vogue by the 1950s. To this generation, the three-bedroom bungalow was a major goal and living in an old house, the furthest from chic. Nevertheless, the number of young families in Niagara-on-the-Lake did increase following the war.

A number of modest "war houses" were built for veterans on streets adjacent to the Commons or Camp Niagara. These homes seem to fit in well with the older architecture, adding a simple statement to the built heritage of the town. At the same time, a few light industries were established, providing some jobs, but many of these were located on the outskirts. The town never suffered the excessive building booms of other towns across the province and never developed an industrial district.

A basket factory built to service the tender fruit industry was located near the marina and employed a number of locals, but it burned in 1961 and was not replaced. A canning factory built in 1912, used to billet Polish soldiers in

1918 and re-activated following World War I, operated into the early 1950s but finally closed, putting more out of work.

One industry that did thrive for some time revived something for which Niagara had once been famous — boat building. The Sheppard Boat Company, established in 1939, constructed pleasure boats in its shops on the waterfront until finally closing in 1977. Hinterholler Yachts was founded in 1964, becoming C and C Yachts in 1969. In its heyday it produced over 500 luxury craft annually, but it too became a victim of financial difficulties. While it seemed to be on the road to recovery in the early 90s, it was finally closed following a fire in the factory in 1994.

The most enduring of these postwar industries is Genaire, a manufacturer of technology for the aircraft industry. It operates from the airport and from a wartime structure built near historic Butler's Barracks.

Several other important parts of today's community were built within a few years of the end of the war. The old high school had become much too crowded. It was closed and for a while the students were bused into the city, but soon the modern Niagara District High School was built. In 1948, Parliament Oak Public School replaced the nineteenth-century brick building used for decades. Parliament Oak was built adjacent to the remains of a huge oak tree under which local legend declared that the first Parliament of Upper Canada met in the summer of 1793. The old high school, which stood beside the Niagara Historical Society Museum, was linked to and became part of the

*Niagara Historical Society Museum*

museum, while the large brick public school has been converted into apartments.

The earliest hospital in Niagara-on-the-Lake was built 200 years ago as part of Fort George. The military continued to operate a hospital on the Commons until 1870 for the troops in garrison but not for the general public. Civilians were tended in their own homes by doctors during the nineteenth century. However, late in 1919, a "Cottage Hospital" was established on Gate Street, moving to Queen Street the following year. The current hospital, which has undergone considerable change in the past decade, was part of the postwar civic building boom. It opened its doors in 1951.

While there was some construction in town following the war, it was not nearly as extensive as that in many other Ontario towns. Thankfully, Niagara-on-the-Lake was spared the postwar modernization movement that replaced so many heritage structures in Ontario with modern structures. This was partially

*Breakenridge House, 392 Mississauga Street*

because its citizens had a strong sense of the value of their heritage but mainly because few could afford the cost of renovation or new construction. In many respects, poverty preserved Niagara-on-the-Lake long enough for a few people with money and vision to recognize the value of the town's old buildings.

## The Restoration Movement

The historic importance of the town had always been acknowledged. The official opening of the restored Fort George and Navy Hall on June 8, 1950, emphasized the town's proud past. The site restoration had been completed in 1939 by the Niagara Parks Commission, but the official opening was delayed by the war. Now tourists were coming by car to see the fort, but merchants lamented that few tourists came into town to spend their money. Tourism was not yet an important stimulus to the economy of Niagara-on-the-Lake.

In the mid-1950s, several of the town's residents realized that the town's heritage was its most valuable asset. These people had the resources to do something about it. Several old buildings were threatened with demolition; the fear of losing this heritage seemed to electrify the group. Mrs. Kathleen Drope, Frank Hawley and the Oppenheimer family from Buffalo were among these restoration pioneers. A movement to save and restore got underway. While the restorers took pride in their efforts, others gave them sidelong glances, questioning the sanity of people who would pour money into these dusty old houses when new construction would be cheaper. Frank Hawley's beautifully restored "Breakenridge House," built around 1818, was one of the first houses to be rescued. Hawley bought the house in 1953 and began carefully returning the structure to its early glory. Some local wags, wondering why anyone should go to so much trouble and expense, dubbed the building "Hawley's Folly." The results of his labour, however, were stunning. With restored window sashes, a re-shingled roof, repaired siding repainted in heritage colours and other improvements, the old house was much more elegant than any new construction. People took notice and the restoration movement continued to attract attention.

*78 Prideaux Street*

buildings recognized as being of historical importance was astounding. Stokes's work and his invaluable advice led to further restoration not only of residential but of commercial buildings. Stokes restored a neglected house on King Street for himself and his wife; both continue to contribute to the town's preservation. Their house stands as a testament to restoration at its purest.

The Niagara Foundation was instrumental in the restoration of the courthouse and the Niagara Apothecary, Ontario's oldest continuously run pharmacy at the time the work was completed in 1971. Since then the foundation has continued to raise funds and assist in the preservation of the town. In the 1970s, the town appointed a Local Architectural Conservation Advisory Committee (LACAC), one of Ontario's first, which was made up of a group of interested citizens, including Stokes, that would advise the town on heritage matters.

Owners of old buildings were strongly encouraged to preserve them. On the urging of the foundation and the advice of LACAC, Niagara Town Council designated the main historic area of the old town as a Heritage District under the Ontario Heritage Act. As a result, still more houses and businesses were restored to their nineteenth-century appearance. Today any changes to the exteriors of these designated buildings are carefully monitored to ensure that their heritage character is respected. Neon signs, overhead signs and other modern commercial devices that would compromise the nineteenth-century streetscapes are banned.

*Shops on Queen Street*

The first restorations spurred further work and further interest. Craftsmen dusted off old skills and other restoration experts relocated to town. Soon Niagara-on-the-Lake had the knowledge and the ability to carefully bring its historic buildings back to their initial splendour.

In 1962, a town planning board meeting debated the value of preserving the town's heritage. Soon afterwards, a group of ten concerned residents formed a foundation to ensure the preservation of town landmarks. The Niagara Foundation raised funds to purchase and restore buildings and assumed a strong advocacy role. The federal government was persuaded to conduct an inventory of heritage structures, and Canada's leading restoration architect, Peter J. Stokes, was hired to carry out the survey. The number of

## Rebirth of Tourism

Another important step in the renaissance of Niagara-on-the-Lake began in 1962 when a small group organized a summer theatre to present the plays of George Bernard Shaw. The theatre became increasingly popular, soon attracting audiences from Toronto and Buffalo. Within a few years, albeit with its share of controversy and some criticism by local residents, the Shaw Festival was established as a professional theatre company. It now operates three theatres during its seven-month season — the Festival Theatre, the Royal George Theatre and its original Court House Theatre. It has become known throughout the world and is one of the driving forces in the old town.

Niagara-on-the-Lake's efforts to conserve the past were unusual enough at the time that the town received a fair bit of media attention. Tourists came in increasing numbers and word of the beauty of the town spread. The Shaw began to flourish. By the early 1970s, while many residents welcomed the stimulation of the economy through tourist dollars, others feared that the influx of visitors would have an adverse effect on the town's quiet, historic ambiance. A number of people who had moved to the town and had

*The Gazebo, Queen's Royal Park*

extensively restored their homes had been attracted by the peaceful beauty they found in the area. They feared that their new-found lifestyle would be compromised if the town became too busy.

*Lakewinds, 328 Queen Street*

The tourism did affect the town, but in a fortunate way. The service industry grew as more visitors came. The Angel Inn, one of Ontario's oldest, entertained increasing numbers of customers with its pub fare, cold ale and tales of the ghost reputed to haunt the old building. The venerable Moffat Inn again found its rooms full of happy customers. The century-old Prince of Wales Hotel was renovated by new owners and was twice expanded in the mid-1970s and early 1980s, once with less sympathy to the original architecture and later with façades added to the additions to blend in with the original structure. In 1999, the hotel was again given a major face-lift, a $15-million renovation, to make it the region's most elegant inn, closely rivalled by the other hotels owned by enterprising hotelier Si Wai Lai.

Niagara-on-the-Lake now has a number of first-class dining and accommodation facilities, including a variety of fine bed and breakfasts, many in carefully restored period buildings. In some cases, extra revenue earned through B&B operations was used in the expensive job of preserving the buildings in which they were established. By 1999, the town boasted over 200 of these unique accommodations.

An interesting and eclectic mix of merchandise became available in the restored buildings of Queen Street to serve the town's visitors. The owners of town businesses, some of which, like the Niagara Home Bakery and Greaves Jams, had been on the street for decades, took pride in the historic business district and worked with LACAC to bring old buildings back to their original character.

## Blending in the New

It is not as though Niagara-on-the-Lake simply preserved the old. In-filling and new construction in the heritage district, essential in any growing town, were done to harmonize with the existing architecture. The building in which the Old Niagara Bookshop operates, reconstructed in 1981, now appears as though it has been here since the early days of the town. Other new construction, like the Shaw Court, was designed to give the appearance of original architecture, while a few other relatively recent structures, such as the Post Office, are modern designs built to complement the streetscape. A stroll down Queen Street is not only an enjoyable shopping experience but a walk through Ontario's retail history, with buildings representing all periods from the 1820s to the 1990s. All blend together to give a feeling of the past.

Not only did businesses flourish, but so did the housing industry. Niagara has always worked its magic on visitors, many of whom come once and decide to become permanent or at least summer residents. As tourism grew in the 1970s and 80s, so did the number of people who wished to settle here. Plentiful jobs in the service industry allowed children of older residents to stay in town instead of moving away to larger centres for employment. The demand for housing continues, and a number of new projects have been built to house the growing population. Vacant lots became building lots and a new subdivision, Garrison Village, was constructed on the edge of town. This has been followed by a number of housing developments. In the 1990s a new sewage treatment plant allowed a great deal of expansion. Condominiums and houses sprang up, many of which were built to reflect nineteenth-century architecture. One such development, The

Village, allows only houses designed by selected architects to reflect building styles and streetscapes of old Niagara. Some of these new buildings appear to be well over a century old, yet an orchard grew on the site until 1997.

## Guardians of Heritage

None of Niagara's later developments has occurred without controversy. Niagara-on-the-Lake's residents are passionate about the preservation of their town, and anything that could compromise the integrity of its heritage has been vigorously challenged. The amalgamation of the Old Town with the communities of Virgil, Queenston, St. Davids and the rest of the township in 1970 created fears that the heritage of Niagara-on-the-Lake would not be respected. Citizens also vigorously opposed the loss of part of the Commons to the construction of two seniors' residences and the Shaw Festival Theatre. Plans to construct large buildings such as the Queen's Landing and the King's Point Condominium were challenged at the Ontario Municipal Board level.

The heritage crusaders of the town ensure that any development is carefully considered so that the town will retain its heritage character. Groups such as the Niagara Foundation and LACAC work more behind the scenes to aid preservation. The Friends of Fort George assists Parks Canada in telling the stirring stories of the town's past, while the Niagara Conservancy serves a strong advocacy role to challenge any developments that could have an impact on the heritage of the town. The Historic Society similarly helps to preserve and present the colourful past, with the museum serving as a repository for the town's treasures while the library maintains a wonderfully helpful research facility. During the War of 1812, the area was largely defended by

*The Commons in spring*

its volunteers. That spirit survives to this day in the many battles to save our past.

The cultural and historic nature of the town has drawn artists, writers, poets, actors, historians, craftsmen and a variety of talented people. Artists Trish Romance and

Inniskillin Wines, estate wineries developed high standards for their Vintners Quality Assurance (VQA)-certified products. High-quality vinifera grapes have been adapted to the local growing conditions and with talent and hard work, several estate wineries have walked away with a plethora of international awards. The wines are a good symbol for the town — elegant and world class.

* * *

The last half of the twentieth century has been characterized in Niagara by heritage conservation and culture. Although it tended to develop much in the fashion of other small Ontario towns

*Vineyards near Niagara-on-the-Lake*

Angie Strauss have developed successful businesses selling their artwork. Other artists, including Magdalena Titian, Karoly Veress and Campbell Scott, find inspiration in their adopted town. In the 1990s a group of citizens formed a committee to restore the old waterworks building and establish the Pumphouse Art Gallery, where works by many local artists are featured. Art lessons are regularly offered. Niagara's fascinating mix of residents work together to make the town one that breathes heritage, quality and elegance.

In recent years, vintners have taken advantage of the region's mild microclimate, similar to that of the great wine-growing regions of France and Germany. While grapes have been grown here for wine since the early nineteenth-century, it took people with vision to make this into a true wine region. Led primarily by Donald Ziraldo of

immediately after World War II, it remained economically depressed and did not develop as radically. Old buildings were saved long enough to allow some individuals with a good eye for beauty to begin a restoration movement that continues to thrive. The development of the Shaw Festival and the influx of artists into town have given the historic town a cultured flavour, and this combination of culture and heritage has proven popular with visitors. Niagara-on-the-Lake has a very strong tourism industry, which has proven to be the economic saviour of the town.

# 7

# THE SHAW FESTIVAL AND THEATRE IN NIAGARA

O ne of the defining elements of Niagara-on-the-Lake, along with its preserved historic buildings, is the Shaw Festival, a theatre company specializing in the plays of George Bernard Shaw and his contemporaries. The Shaw Festival started out modestly as a way to attract more tourists to the town, bolstering the economy, providing jobs and perhaps contributing to the preservation of the town's heritage. The productions at the three Shaw theatres were not the first plays performed in Niagara-on-the-Lake, however. Amateur theatre has a place in the town's past.

## Theatre on the Frontier

From the earliest days of Niagara, theatre played a role in the social life of the community. Officers of the British army in garrison at Fort George and later at Butler's Barracks entertained the community from time to time with a limited repertoire of comedies, farces and melodramas. Some of the titles are intriguing with *John Bull*, *The Heir at Law*, and the *Irish Tutor* remaining popular offerings over a couple of decades. The farce *Modern Antiques* has a curious ring

considering that it was presented as early as 1809 by the garrison of Quebec City, while the comedy *The Honey Moon* was performed here long before neighbouring Niagara Falls became known as "the Honeymoon Capital."

Throughout the nineteenth century and into the twentieth, local amateurs put on a number of theatrical presentations. This was nothing remarkable, however, and typical of any small town in Ontario. The vision and initiative of a few people would soon change that.

*The Royal George*

## The Beginnings of the Shaw Festival

Brian Doherty, a successful lawyer who had moved to Niagara from Toronto in 1955, was the driving force behind the establishment of the Shaw. Doherty had always shown a keen interest in theatre and had been involved in it at several levels. His production of *Father Malachy's Miracle* did very well on Broadway in 1937–38 and he had been instrumental in the development of theatre in Canada, being largely responsible for the Straw Hat Players, the Red Barn Theatre and the New World Theatre. Over the years he had developed an appreciation of the works of George Bernard Shaw, whose plays were performed in Canada on occasion — but to mixed reviews.

On Doherty's arrival in Niagara-on-the-Lake he quickly became fascinated with the history of the town. He served as the president of the Niagara Historical Society from 1959 to 1961 and his social circle included a number of those who were actively restoring old buildings in Niagara-on-the-Lake. At that time, everyone realized that something must be done to ensure the preservation of the town, which was still sunk in economic difficulty.

The idea of establishing a theatre was developed in a scene that could have been lifted from one of Shaw's plays. Doherty and a small group of people were gathered for coffee and drinks at the Niagara-on-the-Lake home of Jean Marsh. Talk turned to heritage preservation and steps that could be taken to stimulate interest in the old town, to boost tourism and therefore improve the economic prospects of the place. In Doherty's book on the first years of the Shaw Festival, *Not Bloody Likely*, he recalls saying, "Let's do something for the town we love, something we believe in." The idea of theatre was suggested and immediately Doherty exclaimed, "Shaw! Shaw would be wonderful."

The question of a location for the productions was discussed and immediately the old courthouse came to mind. On the third floor of the building was a large meeting room with a rudimentary stage. The room was well lit and could hold a couple of hundred people. A second room was large enough for dressing rooms, storage and the other requirements for a theatre.

Within a day, one of the guests at that now-famous party had arranged for use of the courthouse and had called a meeting to set up a committee to develop a Shaw Festival. Doherty was nominated as the chairman of the committee and also found himself assuming the roles of artistic director and producer. The committee's major supporters were among the most active in the heritage preservation movement.

*The Court House Theatre*

Early in 1962 the group set to work to organize that summer's bill. Doherty recruited Maynard Burgess, a local actor/director and they decided to present two productions — *Candida* and *Don Juan in Hell* from *Man and Superman* — in eight performances between June 29 and August 11. The event was to be called "Salute to Shaw." Although the intention was to establish a professional theatre, the decision was made that no one would draw a salary that first summer. Burgess would direct a cast drawn from the community and from the Welland Little Theatre. There would still be expenses for costumes, set materials, programs and publicity. An energetic group set out to find the money to make the "Salute" possible.

The first work presented was *Don Juan in Hell*, with Burgess playing the role of the Devil and directing the production. It was done as a reading, which required few props and few actors for the roles. Appropriate perhaps to the setting for the play, a heat wave turned the courthouse into a sauna on opening night. Doherty's committee raced all over town borrowing electric fans to provide the audience with some comfort, but to little avail. In spite of the discomfort, the audience of close to 200 enjoyed the play immensely.

*Christopher Newton and Betty Leighton in* Heartbreak House, *1964*

Meanwhile, rehearsals for *Candida* carried on.

The second program in the "Salute" required costumes and sets and a larger group of actors. The set was enhanced with antique furniture borrowed from friends of the Shaw committee. Again, through the hard work of volunteers, everything was prepared. *Candida* opened on July 27 to a larger audience. These performances sold many of the residents of Niagara-on-the-Lake on the idea of theatre in the town.

The committee quickly decided to proceed with the establishment of a Shaw Festival, based on the response to this first fledgling season of eight performances. The theatre would be put on a more professional basis; some basic amenities would be added to the Court House "Theatre" and the company would hire an artistic director. Andrew Allan was persuaded to give Niagara-on-the-Lake a try. Allan was a well-known CBC Radio producer/director who had received his initial training at the University of Toronto's Hart House Theatre, as had Doherty. Allan recruited actor/director Sean Mulcahy and they began planning the next season. Private donations helped offset some of the costs

associated with salaries and theatre improvements, but the Festival still needed a source of income to make the whole thing possible. A plan for a pre-season performance in Toronto and the committee's hard work to sell out the performance provided the necessary capital. The second season was launched.

This second season in 1963 was extended to three productions to run for three weeks. Featured were *You Never Can Tell, Androcles and the Lion* and the two one-act plays *How He Lied to Her Husband* and *The Man of Destiny*. The sets had to be built in the parking lot behind the courthouse, and there was little money available for material for props or costumes, but thanks to the town's longstanding support from volunteers, the productions were of a relatively high quality. *Androcles*, with its large cast, relied on a number of unpaid residents acting in the minor roles.

Support for the Shaw and the success of the first two seasons encouraged the group to formalize their operations. In that second season they incorporated as a nonprofit organization with a board of directors and more formal planning sessions.

The next two seasons, still under the artistic directorship of Allan, was a time of continued expansion and development so that the 1964 season saw

Heartbreak House, *1964*

the production of four plays over four weeks. In the following year the season was extended to six weeks. In 1964, a young Christopher Newton, who would become the most prolific of the artistic directors of the Shaw after he moved into that position 16 years later, played Hector Hushabye in *Heartbreak House* and Mr. "A" in *Village Wooing*.

In 1965, the Shaw Festival's mandate was subsantially enlarged to allow the performance of plays by Shaw's contemporaries. *The Shadow of a Gunman* by Sean O'Casey was the first non-Shaw performance. Also in that year, Doherty founded the "Shaw Seminar" series in partnership with Brock University. The sceries offered academic insights and rapidly grew to attract scholars and theatre lovers from across Canada. Another major breakthrough that year was a modest Ontario Arts Council grant, which finally allowed the group to operate in the black.

*The Festival Theatre, under construction, 1972*

Niagara-on-the-Lake. Finally, in 1966 it was decided to actually construct a proper theatre, a major financial undertaking but typical of this group's willingness to aim high and take risks to develop the Shaw Festival.

Andrew Allan moved along after the 1965 season and the well-known Canadian actor Barry Morse was cajoled into taking up the reins as artistic director. Morse was an incredibly energetic force who immediately extended the 1966 season to nine weeks, during which the theatre was filled to capacity. He encouraged the Board to seriously investigate building a theatre and in that year the search for a site and the campaign to finance the building was undertaken in earnest. Although Morse stayed only the one season, his energy continued to motivate the builders of the Shaw Festival.

In 1967, Canada's Centennial year, Paxton Whitehead became the Shaw's artistic director. Whitehead was a young English actor/director who had emigrated to Canada two years earlier. He continued to expand the Festival's offerings and within four years the season had been lengthened to 12 weeks. The theatre's professionalism was improved by the hiring of a set designer, costume designer and general manager to handle the business side of things.

The search for an appropriate site for a new theatre continued and brought with it a wave of controversy. The committee looked at Queen's Royal Park where the elegant Queen's Royal Hotel once stood, but the town of Niagara-on-the-Lake refused to sell the land. The federal

## The Shaw Expands

The first few years had been so successful that it soon became obvious that a permanent theatre building would be needed. The old Brock movie house (now the Shaw's Royal George Theatre) was considered but rejected when the Board realized that the required repairs to make the old building operable would be unsupportable. Toronto entrepreneur Ed Mirvish offered to move the whole festival to his Royal Alexandra Theatre but that was rejected by the Board which was, after all, doing all of this to benefit government offered land beside Fort Mississauga, but this would have meant the cancellation of the agreement with Canada's oldest golf club, which leased the land from the government for the Niagara-on-the-Lake golf course. Understandably, this met with howls of embittered protest. It became obvious that few were willing to sacrifice heritage to develop the theatre. The government listened and withdrew the offer of land on the Mississauga Commons. Finally, the search committee settled on the parking lot behind the courthouse as a suitable spot. The town of Niagara-on-the-Lake was prepared to sign a long-term lease with the Board to allow construction of the theatre here.

Meanwhile, Calvin Rand, scion of a Buffalo family that had been involved in Niagara-on-the-Lake since the late nineteenth century, led the drive to find the finances to build the new theatre. Rand had been an important part of the Shaw Festival from the start and was just the man to find the money needed. By 1971 he had lined up private and corporate donations and grants from both provincial and federal governments amounting to $500,000 each. Ron Thom, a Toronto architect who was sympathetic to the heritage nature of the town, was chosen from a long list to design the new facility.

When preliminary illustrations of Thom's design showing the theatre behind the courthouse were made public, it became clear to the town's many heritage advocates that the theatre would compromise the historic integrity of the period buildings surrounding it — including the courthouse itself. Again a huge protest was launched and many fiery

*The Festival Theatre*

letters were written to editors, to the Shaw directors and to all levels of government. The Shaw's search for a suitable location was dividing the very town it had been founded to help. Animosity over the whole issue of space for a theatre grew. The Board backed down from the idea of building the theatre behind the courthouse and the town council breathed a sigh of relief now that it realized how unpopular that concept was with many townspeople.

Finally a site was found on the corner of Wellington Street and the road romantically known as Queen's Parade. The new location, part of the Commons, was owned by Parks Canada, which negotiated a long-term lease with the Shaw Festival. Even this new site met with controversy. The Commons was regarded as sacred land, a green space on the edge of Niagara that is valued as open space to be used by all residents. The development of a part of that land represented a dangerous precedent; fears exist to this day that the land will all eventually be sold off for development. In spite of a new wave of protest and an appeal to the Ontario Municipal Board, the Shaw Festival continued with its plans. Thom's designs for the courthouse location were revised and by the beginning of 1972 all was ready for construction to begin.

The sod was turned in the spring and work began on Thom's impressive design. The Festival Theatre, as it was to be called, would be built of materials that blend in with the architecture of Niagara, even though the structure would be absolutely modern in style. Careful landscaping would make the theatre's surroundings into a natural paradise, blending its cultivated gardens into the more natural landscape of the Commons, which bounded it on two sides. The theatre itself featured dressing rooms, prop rooms, costume workshops, meeting rooms, a library, a large tiered lobby, administrative offices and an acoustically balanced 861-seat theatre, a far cry from the early days in the old Court House Theatre.

The Festival Theatre was completed on the morning of its scheduled opening in June 1973. The new theatre was an instant hit with staff, actors and audiences. The additional facilities allowed the ambitious presentation of four demanding plays during a 15-week season. The Shaw had finally "arrived": and among

*Prime Minister Pierre Trudeau and Margaret Trudeau chat with Festival founder, Brian Doherty, 1973*

the new theatre's guests in the inaugural week of operation were Prime Minister Pierre Trudeau, Prime Minister Indira Gandhi of India and Ontario's Premier William Davis. The most illustrious visitors came on June 28 when Her Majesty Queen Elizabeth II and H.R.H. the Duke of Edinburgh attended a special performance of *You Never Can Tell*. The royal couple honoured the company by going backstage to greet the cast following the performance.

The Shaw continued to expand, going on tour, filling the courthouse (which was retained) and the new Festival Theatre with appreciative patrons and developing a reputation in Canada and the United States for the quality of its presentations. As more patrons came to Niagara-on-the-Lake, tourism flourished and the entire business community began to prosper by the mid-1970s. The mix of history, restored buildings and theatre established Niagara-on-the-Lake as a beautiful and elegant cultured town in the eyes of thousands of visitors.

Paxton Whitehead had seen the Shaw Festival progress from a modest company using part of the old courthouse to a professional group with an impressive modern theatre. He moved on, however, at the end of the 1977 season. By that time, the Shaw was presenting five plays over a 15-week season, a far cry from the original eight performances of the "Salute to Shaw." Whitehead's position was temporarily filled by Richard Kirschner and Leslie Yeo over the next two seasons while the search continued for a permanent artistic director.

## A New Artistic Director

Christopher Newton was convinced to take the helm following the 1979 season. Newton had been the artistic director of the Vancouver Playhouse since 1972 and the founding artistic director of Theatre Calgary from 1968 to 1971. He has been the key to the modern Shaw Festival's success. Another crucial element was added in the person of Cameron Porteous as head of design. Over

*Colombe Demers and Gordon Rand in* Lady Windermere's Fan, *1998*

developing an "ensemble" of actors, an extended family of artists who would regard the Shaw as their home, even during seasons when they had no roles in Shaw productions or when working at other theatres. He demanded excellence and engineered programs to help actors develop professionally. In 1985, the Shaw Academy was started with a series of workshops designed to help actors hone their skills. Today, the Academy has been expanded to reach out to the public with the company of the Shaw Festival providing fascinating and instructive insights into theatre to adults and students. Newton's work is recognized in the description of the Shaw Festival by The Cambridge Guide to Theatre as "home to one of the finest acting ensembles in North America."

the next two decades, Newton and company would bring the Shaw to the height of excellence.

Newton had acted in a couple of plays in the Festival's early years in the old courthouse and apparently had been left with a somewhat negative memory of the occasions. He was also anything but enthusiastic about Shaw as a playwright. Nevertheless, he agreed to become the artistic director but undoubtedly had few illusions concerning any sort of lengthy stay with the theatre. He entered the job, however, with the enthusiasm, wit and creativity for which he is so well known and immediately established a pattern that has ably led the company into the twenty-first century. His first season featured eleven productions in three theatres. Within a year, the season was expanded to five months. Newton's non-traditional interpretations of Shaw initially raised some eyebrows among the more conservative Shavians but within a short time a huge and loyal following came to appreciate his artistic presentations of Shaw and his contemporaries. Newton has been able to make their plays relevant to today's world.

Newton believed strongly in the importance of a theatre

## Success

Throughout the evolution of the Shaw Festival, volunteers and supporters have been most important. Corporate donors

Major Barbara, *1998*

and hundreds of private members help keep the organization financially stable. The dedicated members of the Shaw Guild help organize a variety of special events that allow continued expansion of the Festival. Among the more unusual of the latter is the Shaw Boxing event, an exclusive black-tie fundraiser held annually at the Royal York Hotel in Toronto. Bernard Shaw was a fan of boxing and would have felt right at home sitting ringside at the event.

The Shaw has experienced financial highs and lows during its history. When Newton arrived, the theatre was in debt, but this was turned around for several years. Following the recession of the 1980s, the Festival was again operating in the red but this was reversed beginning in 1996. The magical combination of Newton's artistic professionalism and insistence on excellence along with the business acumen of Managing Director Colleen Blake built the Festival in the 90s into a very lucrative venture with an ever-expanding season and sold-out performances. In the 1998 season, 321,000 tickets were sold for a total revenue of $16.8 million.

The Shaw offers a complete theatre environment with a number of interesting innovations added over the years. Lunchtime theatre and a special Reading Series provide audiences with shorter presentations. Sunday brunch concerts are performed by members of the Shaw company. Visits to the theatre are enriched by backstage tours, pre-show chats, question-and-answer sessions and other offerings by the ensemble, meant to give theatre patrons a better understanding of the art. Educational programs for

*Simon Bradbury in* The Lady's Not for Burning, *1998*

school children and seminars for adults and post-secondary students provide an important academic service.

Today, the Shaw Festival operates from mid-April to the end of November. The stages are dark only on Mondays. The three theatres offer different experiences to their audiences. The original Court House Theatre, much improved since the early days of the Festival, seats 324 people in an intimate setting. Plays that require a great deal of audience concentration are performed here. The 861-seat Festival Theatre, described by the Shaw as their "flagship," is where the larger productions are presented, those requiring what Newton refers to as "size and grandeur." The Royal George Theatre, restored and beautifully decorated in Victorian elegance, seats 328 and presents lighter plays, musicals, murder mysteries and the popular lunchtime theatre productions.

\* \* \*

The Shaw has become an integral part of the historic town of Niagara-on-the-Lake. It is difficult to imagine the town without the Shaw Festival and its company. The Shaw, combined with the rich history, old forts and restored residential streets of the town make Niagara-on-the-Lake unique. The Festival has helped a variety of businesses flourish: the town is well endowed with fine hotels, picturesque shops, superb restaurants and a variety of businesses catering to visitors. Certainly there are few other towns of 5,000 souls that welcome as many visitors. Brian Doherty's vision of using high-quality theatre to help the town has been fulfilled.

# AFTERWORD

Niagara-on-the-Lake's rich and colourful history is immediately evident to all who visit. Houses and buildings dating back to the early nineteenth century are lovingly restored and cared for by a heritage-conscious public. The streetscapes still resemble the way they looked over a hundred years ago. Ardent horticulturalists and the town's gardening experts ensure that the town is a glory of plants and flowers. Guides today point out where princes have stayed, where Confederate president Jefferson Davis lived following the collapse of the Confederacy, where U.S. presidents walked, where Isaac Brock commanded and where a who's who of past personalities, larger than life, once lived and worked. Maybe they still do. The town is filled with stories of

*The Commons*

strange sightings and other ghostly tales.

Niagara-on-the-Lake is a town of superlatives. It was the first capital and had the first newspaper and first library in Ontario. Fort George was the headquarters of the British army in Ontario at the time of the War of 1812. The act passed here under John Graves Simcoe that resulted in the abolition of slavery was the first such legislation in the British Empire. In the 1990s it was named by the international "Communities in Bloom" committee as "Canada's Prettiest Town." It is hard to disagree with that sentiment.

The nineteenth-century historian William Kirby said it best when he wrote in the 1890s that "Niagara is as near Heaven as any town whatever." Over a century later, his words ring true.

# *Appendix 1*

# THREE TOURS OF THE TOWN

## TOUR ONE
### *Stately restored houses and the museum*

This walking tour begins in the Fort George parking lot and explores primarily stately homes.

It goes past the Shaw Festival Theatre, the Prince of Wales Hotel, the museum, part of Queen Street, the Queen's Landing Hotel and back to the Fort in a 20 block walk. With a few hotels and restaurants along the way, there are opportunities to stop for refreshments or a meal during the walk. With the town's convenient street grid system it is simple to cut the tour short if time is at a premium and return to the starting point without getting lost.

Starting from the Fort George parking lot, head along Queen's Parade into town. The name Queen's Parade harkens back to the days of Camp Niagara when the large open field on your left, "the Commons," was a large military training centre for Canadian militia.

***1. Shaw Festival Theatre, 1973*** – The 861-seat Festival Theatre is the headquarters of the Shaw Festival. Built in 1973, it was designed by Canadian architect Ron Thom as a modern theatre featuring modern architecture but with materials and landscaping which blend the structure into the cultural and natural landscape of Niagara-on-the-Lake. This is one of three theatres owned by the Shaw.

***2. Niagara General Hospital, 1951***
This was not the town's first hospital but the first structure built as a hospital. Once offering full services, it was threatened by hospital restructuring and the emergency department was closed. It is undergoing a revival with chronic care beds, three doctors' offices and various clinics held.

Proceed across Wellington Street. Queen's Parade now becomes Picton Street.

***3. St. Vincent de Paul Roman Catholic Church, Picton Street, 1834 and 1965***
To your right is St. Vincent de Paul built in 1834. Note the Gothic Revival elements such as the pointed windows. The church was expanded in 1965 with the rounded addition and spire but the original structure of the church is maintained.

***4. The Moffat Inn, 60 Picton Street, circa 1835***
The Moffat has been in continuous operation as a hostelry for the past 165 years. It is a frame building covered in stucco, a nineteenth-century treatment designed to make it more substantial in appearance, to provide insulation and to cut down on maintenance costs.

***5. Simcoe Park, circa 1790***
The park to your right was originally part of the land reserved for the Crown. When the town expanded to this side of King Street after the War of 1812, this space was retained as public land for a park.

Ahead of you, Picton Street becomes Queen Street, the picturesque restored business district of the town. Turn left at King Street.

***6. Prince of Wales Hotel, circa 1882***
The elegant Prince of Wales had a humble beginning as Long's Hotel. It originally served the first tourism boom in Niagara in the late nineteenth century but fell on hard times by the 1920s. It was rescued from ruin in the 1960s and has been greatly expanded in the past thirty years. In 1999 it was completely overhauled and renovated to make it into an opulent Victorian hotel.

### 7. Railway Station, circa 1900

On your right, past Market Street, is the station built for the electric railway which once ran down the centre of King Street. The train left hourly to connect Niagara-on-the-Lake with the city of St. Catharines.

### 8. Firehall, 10 Queen Street, circa 1911

The firehall started life as a livery stable where visitors to town could hire a horse and carriage or could board their horses. In 1912 it became the town's fire hall. Behind the building is a huge siren which once served as an air raid siren.

### 9. Luis House, circa 1913

This frame building was contructed as a restaurant to serve the passengers of the electric railway and the soldiers from the military camp on the Commons. It still caters to the visitors and residents of town.

Turn left across Queen Street to Platoff Street. Notice how the street names in the original part of the town were extended into the "new survey" part of town and given new names. Thus the older Johnson Street becomes Platoff in the expanded area.

### 10. Moore House, 244 King Street, circa 1828

This yellow frame structure which has been a residence during most of its existence did serve briefly as a boarding school in the nineteenth century. It is perhaps the most carefully restored of all of Niagara's buildings with several nineteenth-century additions and embellishments preserved along with the earliest features. The house has an appearance of great antiquity thanks to its many authentic details. Notice the out-of-plumb roof line which was preserved with all of its unevenness by famed restoration architect Peter Stokes.

### 11. Malcomson House, 16 Platoff Street, circa 1840s

The elegant frame Malcomson House was built by one of the founders of the town's public library. The house is oddly asymmetrical with an off-centre front door and window on the side of the building to make the interior parlour more spacious.

### 12. Dover Cottage, 20 Platoff Street, circa 1839

This charming house was built by a local carpenter who was undoubtedly busy working on the rapidly growing town during the building boom of the 1830s. The Dover Cottage was one of the earliest restoration projects in town. The board and batten siding is common in the Niagara area.

### 13. The Public School, 40 Platoff Street, circa 1859

Niagara always had a strong educational community with early schools operated from private residences. This large brick building was built as a public school, serving the town's children until 1948 when the new Parliament Oak School was built nearby.

Turn right onto Davy Street and right again onto Castlereagh.

### 14. Grammar School, 1875

This building was constructed as a high school. It was closed after World War II and replaced by Niagara District High School on Highway 55. In 1972 the old school was joined to Memorial Hall to become part of the Niagara Historical Society Museum.

### 15. Memorial Hall, 1907

Memorial Hall is the oldest building in Ontario built specifically as a museum. In 1972 it was expanded when the Historical Society acquired the old Grammar School and, beginning in 1997, the whole complex was restored and renovated. The museum is well worth a visit, housing valuable and unique artifacts from Niagara's long past. Items such as Isaac Brock's hat and jewelery which once belonged to Laura Secord are on display.

### 16. War Houses, circa 1946

Along Davy Street are a number of smaller houses built to accommodate veterans after World War II.

Cross King Street and turn right along King.

### 17. Veress House, 287 King Street

Note the unique gallery of sculptures on the lawn of artist Karoly Veress's house.

Turn left onto Johnson Street.

### 18. 19 Johnson Street, circa 1830s

This stucco-on-frame house is typical of several such residences built in Niagara-on-the-Lake in the nineteenth century.

### 19. Lawn Bowling Green, circa 1920

After the closing of the Queen's Royal Hotel and its lawn bowling facilities, this became the only lawn bowling green in town. Many local residents enjoy a summer game of "bowls."

**20. Barker Hall, 46 Johnson Street, circa 1831**

Barker Hall is typical of many houses in Ontario. It has a central doorway flanked by a parlour and a keeping room inside, and a central staircase rising from the front door. An unusual feature, seen in a few houses in Niagara-on-the-Lake, is the off-centre doorway to allow for a larger room to the right of the door. This makes the façade asymmetrical in appearance.

**21. Eckersley House, 58 Johnson Street, circa 1833**

Eckersley House shows the attention to detail lavished on buildings by early craftsmen. Note the impressive doorway with sidelights and fanlights which have been carefully restored.

**22. Post House, 95 Johnson Street, 1835**

The red brick building on your right was built by mason James Blair who maintained a brickyard near the house. The structure stands as a good ad for Blair's brick supply business and his skill as a mason. Large windows make the building bright and airy. A relatively rare dated keystone over the door is a boon for present-day historians. The house was one of Niagara's early post offices.

**23. Vanderlip House, 96 Johnson Street, circa 1816**

The Vanderlip House was one of the first built after the War of 1812 to replace the houses burned in 1813. It was built as a one-and-a-half-storey structure, taxed at the time of construction at the same rate as a one-storey house, considerably less than the tax on two full storeys. The windows on the second level at the front of the house are later additions. For many years this house was rumoured to be much older, one of the few survivors of the War of 1812.

**24. Stocking House, 118 Johnson Street, pre-1836**

The Jared Stocking House was known as the Sign of the Crown Inn in 1836 and was once owned by hotelier William Moffat, builder of the Moffat Inn. Early travellers noted the large numbers of taverns in Niagara during this period.

**25. Varey's Terrace, 117–119 Johnson Street, circa 1840s**

This red row house was built by entrepreneur George Varey to house workers of the Niagara Harbour and Dock Company. We are fortunate that a building with humble beginnings has survived and has been faithfully preserved.

**26. Greenlees House, 135 Johnson Street, circa 1822**

Another very early postwar house, it shares an asymmetrical centre hallway plan with several other houses from the same period in the town's history. One wonders if the same builder was involved in their construction or if the owners simply liked the idea of having one larger room on the ground floor.

**27. Ralph Clement House, 144 Johnson Street, circa 1840s**

This substantial red brick home has the same type of generous window treatment as the Post House built a few years earlier by mason Blair. The Clement House was likely built by Blair using bricks from his supply yard.

Turn right on Gate Street.

**28. McMonigle House, 240 Gate Street, circa 1818**

The McMonigle House is another of Niagara's earliest houses, built of frame and board following the War of 1812.

**29. Saltbox House, 223 Gate Street, circa 1850s**

On the left is a simple but beautiful saltbox style cottage which has been restored to its mid-nineteenth century charm.

Proceed to Queen Street.

**30. Gate House Hotel, 142 Queen Street, circa 1900**

The Gate House Hotel was built during Niagara's first tourism boom on the site of John Wilson's Tavern. On this site in 1797 a group of lawyers founded the Law Society of Upper Canada. The tavern was destroyed during the War of 1812.

Cross Queen Street and turn right along Queen.

**31. Candy Safari, 135 Queen Street, circa 1835**

This frame structure was built as a house and shop for shoemaker John Burns. The Gothic-Revival style building has served as a residential and business place throughout its long history.

**32. Angie Strauss Art Gallery, 129 Queen Street, circa 1860s**

Artist Angie Strauss's gallery is one of four old town buildings dating from the period right after the American

Civil War. Like the previous structure and many other buildings in the town's business district it has served as both shop and residence.

### 33. Customs House, 126 Queen Street, circa 1825
Notice the Coat of Arms over the building on the other side of Queen Street. This marks the Customs House which was built as a residence and government office. The early use of a Regency style for the structure shows that the government was at the cutting edge of style in the 1820s. It has been restored with a reconstructed coat of arms adorning its front façade.

Turn left onto Victoria Street.

### 34. Bank of Montreal, 1970
The bank building at the corner of Queen and Victoria was designed to blend in with the town's restored streetscape.

### 35. Wilson House, 177 Victoria Street, circa 1816
This one-and-a-half-storey frame building with five bay front was constructed in 1816 for hotelier John Wilson. The central stairway is flanked by two very well lit rooms on the ground floor.

Turn right on Prideaux Street.

### 36. Thomas Burke House, 94 Prideaux Street, circa 1826
Burke's large clapboard house was operated as one of Niagara's many inns and taverns in the 1850s. Niagara's role as district centre meant that anyone doing official business in the town's courts often had to stay overnight.

### 37. Davidson-Campbell House, 87 Prideaux Street, circa 1845
This house was built by master carpenter John Davidson in 1845. It was enlarged and redecorated in the 1860s with mid-Victorian embellishments which were preserved in the building's restoration.

### 38. Hiscott House, 78 Prideaux Street, circa 1817
The impressive red brick Hiscott House was built in the Georgian style just after the end of the War of 1812. The wooden buildings of the first town were burned so easily that many chose more fireproof brick when they rebuilt. Bricks had also become more plentiful and less expensive.

### 39. Kerr House, 69 Prideaux Street, circa 1815
Dr. Robert Kerr, surgeon of the British Indian Department, built this brick house on the site of his earlier residence, burned in 1813 by the American Army. The foundations of the original house were incorporated in this replacement.

### 40. Promenade House, 55 Prideaux Street, circa 1820
Another imposing brick house, the Promenade, was owned and operated as an inn after 1846 by the same tavern keeper who built the Angel Inn on Market Street. Two of the previous residents had been principals in the formation of the Niagara Harbour and Dock Company.

### 41. Stewart House, 42 Prideaux Street, circa 1830
This is one of several beautifully restored brick homes for which Prideaux Street is noted. The impressive arcading on the front of the house is one of the best examples of the bricklayer's art. The interior of the house features a decorative archway and a sweeping curved stairway.

### 42. Masonic Hall, 153 King Street, circa 1816
To the right is an early building reputedly contructed at the end of the War of 1812 from material salvaged from the burned town. The structure served several uses including a military barracks before becoming a Masonic Temple in the 1860s. Today it continues in use by the Freemasons while serving as the Chamber of Commerce office for the town.

Cross King Street and continue on Byron Street.

### 43. St. Mark's Rectory, 17 Byron Street, 1858
To your left is Niagara's only example of a Tuscan-style villa. The pressed buff brick building was constructed as a rectory in 1858 and served that purpose for over 125 years. Recently it has been restored by the Niagara Foundation and is now leased as a private residence.

### 44. St. Marks Anglican Church, circa 1805 and 1843
St. Mark's was first constructed in 1805 to serve the Church of England's congregation in the town and to serve as the garrison church for Fort George. It was burned in 1813 and restored following the war. The church was enlarged in 1843 and still serves an active congregation. Surrounding the church is a cemetery which initially served all denominations until other burying grounds were established. Many of Niagara's important early citizens are interred here and the cemetery has become a popular spot for visitors interested in our past. Across the road is the cemetery serving the Roman

Catholic population. Within an enclosure are the graves of many Polish soldiers who died during World War I while training at Camp Niagara.

### 45. Queen's Landing Hotel, 155 Byron Street, 1980

This imposing four-diamond hotel, one of the area's finest, was built under a cloud of controversy. It was deemed to be too overpowering for Niagara's skyline but was approved in spite of that. Today it seems to fit with the character of the town and grows less intrusive with age.

### 46. Fort George, circa 1796

Fort George was the headquarters of the British Army in Southern Ontario before the War of 1812. It was burned, captured and occupied by American forces in 1813, retaken and rebuilt by the British later in the year, abandoned in the 1830s and in ruins by the beginning of the twentieth century. It was reconstructed in the 1930s and now welcomes thousands of visitors who come to enjoy its rich history and colourful program presented by staff in authentically recreated War of 1812 uniforms. The Powder Magazine in the fort, the only survivor from those times, was built in 1796 and is the oldest building in Niagara.

# TOUR TWO
## The restored shopping district

This tour begins at the courthouse parking lot and proceeds down Queen Street, the restored business district with commercial buildings and houses going back 180 years. Visitors have the option of walking back on the other side of Queen Street or following the tour down to the riverfront, past restored houses, Queen's Royal Park and then back up King Street, past the Chamber of Commerce building and back to the start. The entire tour is about twelve blocks but visitors returning along Queen Street will cover only eight blocks.

From the courthouse parking lot proceed along Market Street to Regent Street.

### 1. The Angel Inn, 46 Market Street, circa 1825

The Angel Inn, originally known as the Sign of the Angel, has served travellers for the past 175 years. It now features a wide selection of beers and ales along with the wines of the Niagara Region. The Angel is reputed to be haunted by the ghost of a War of 1812 soldier who only becomes agitated when the Union Jack does not fly above the door of the Inn.

Turn right onto Regent Street and left on Queen Street. Visitors can stroll along either side of Queen and enjoy the rich collection of heritage buildings on either side.

### 2. The Dee Building, 54–58 Queen Street, circa 1843

This two-storey brick building has held a variety of shops through the ages housing everything from greengrocers to clothing stores. Note the original shopfront facing Regent Street and the impressive transomed doorway. Another shopfront faces Queen Street.

### 3. The Stagecoach, 45 Queen Street, circa 1825

Although the façade of this very early commercial building has evolved over the ages, many interesting original features are still visible in the interior, particularly its beaded ceiling.

### 4. Greaves Jams, 55 Queen Street, circa 1845

A substantial building constructed during the boom of the 1840s around the same time as the Dee Building, this structure retains many of its early features. Note the deep boxed cornices of the hip roof. The entire building was made to last.

### 5. Niagara Home Bakery, 66 Queen Street, circa 1875

Across the street from Greaves Jams, this brick building is one of only four survivors of the decade following Canada's Confederation. The double storefront is entered through a double-leaf door. Extra light is brought in through the glassed transom over the doorway.

### 6. Old Towne Ice Cream Shoppe, 61–63 Queen Street, circa 1948

On the other side of Queen, this one-storey "modern" building was constructed right after World War II before the value of the town's built heritage was fully realized. The owners have added traditional decorative elements to the building so that it now fits in well with its older neighbours such as the building to its right, constructed a century before.

### 7. The Viking Shop, 76 Queen Street, circa 1910

This building was constructed at the height of the first Niagara-on-the-Lake tourism boom prior to World War I.

It is a twentieth-century interpretation of Regency-style architecture, possibly inspired by building elements on the main streets of other towns.

### 8. Taylor's Variety, 64 Queen Street, circa 1900

Taylor's store across the street from the Viking Shop was built in roughly the same period but in a less whimsical, more businesslike style. Like many commercial buildings, it was constructed with a second storey which could be used for offices or as residential space.

### 9. Royal George Theatre, 83 Queen Street, circa 1915

This spot has always been a site of entertainment. The "Kitchener" theatre was built for movies and live vaude-ville acts to entertain the troops from Camp Niagara in 1915. Its name was changed to the "Royal George" and later to the "Brock Cinema." In 1972 it became home to the Canadian Mime Theatre and renovated as the "Royal George." Restored in 1980, it became the third of the Shaw Festival's theatres.

### 10. Bank of Montreal Block, circa 91 Queen Street, 1970

This modern brick structure was purposely built to blend in with the historic streetscapes of Niagara-on-the-Lake.

### 11. Shaw Court, 92 Queen Street, 1997

Opposite the Bank of Montreal is the town's most recent addition, a modern structure but with stylistic features reminiscent of the Victorian age. The bronze statue is of George Bernard Shaw who never actually visited the town although his work plays a major role in Niagara-on-the-Lake.

Continue across Victoria Street and along Queen.

### 12. McLelland's West End Store, 106 Queen Street, circa 1835

With the town's rapidly growing population during the shipbuilding boom of the 1830s, this store with its Classic Revival gable front was built as a provisioners — selling groceries, wines and spirits to inhabitants and travellers. Notice the large painted "T" sign of the provisioner. The store was very successful and in 1880 an extension was built beside it at 108 Queen Street. Both structures still house stores servicing residents and visitors and are superbly pre-served examples of Niagara's commercial past.

### 13. Post Offices, 114 Queen and 117 Queen Street, 1950 and 1978

The one-storey concrete block building beside McLelland's buildings was built in 1950 as a modern new post office. Twenty-eight years later, a replacement was built on the other side of Queen Street. Although both buildings are modern, the second brick building blends in well with Niagara's streetscape by attempting to replicate a period structure.

### 14. Gollop House, 118 Queen Street, circa 1830

The Gollop House, a beautiful old frame building, has served as a residence and as shop space during its long history. At one time, a blacksmith lived here and set up his forge in a barn in back. The barn was saved in 1992 and converted into a pleasant shop.

### 15. The Evans Block, 122–124 Queen Street, circa 1840

This block of merchants' shops was built as the town business district expanded in the age of the steamship. The large windows on both floors were designed to let in a great deal of light, suggesting that the upper story was built as office space. Its location next to the custom house would be an ideal location for a customs broker although more research is required to determine the original uses of the second floor.

### 16. Customs Office, 126 Queen Street, circa 1825

The Customs Office, a government building, was unusual in that its Regency design was very stylish at the time of its construction. The need for a customs office indicates the town's role as a major port in the 1820s. The building has been restored, complete with the large painted coat-of-arms surmounting the roof.

### 17. Angie Strauss Gallery, 125–129 Queen Street, circa 1860s

Across Queen Street is one of the few buildings in town sur-viving from the Confederation era. The full-width verandah is an original feature which continues to shade visitors shop-ping in the store, the gallery of artist Angie Strauss.

### 18. Candy Safari, 135 Queen Street, circa 1835

The Candy Safari is in a one-and-a-half-storey Gothic-Revival house which was built as a residence and shop for shoemaker and leatherworker John Burns.

**19. Gate House Hotel, 142 Queen Street, circa 1900**

On this site stood John Wilson's tavern where the Law Society of Upper Canada was founded in 1797, the year that the Provincial Legislature moved from Niagara to Toronto. The society was founded here and established in Toronto where it still oversees Ontario's legal profession.

**20. Rogers House, 157 Queen Street, circa 1817**

The Rogers House is a large six bay house which was built shortly after the end of the war for James Rogers and his family. After 1823 it served as a hotel and tavern. Although it is a frame house, it is covered in stucco fashioned to look like cut stone. The illusion is so effective that many assume that this is a stone building. This exterior treatment is seen on several other buildings in the town.

Turn right on Gate Street.

Strolling down Gate Street with its collection of nineteenth-century buildings with well-maintained gardens is a relaxing experience. The name of the street is somewhat of a mystery with no "gates" evident on early maps of the town.

**21. Oban Inn, corner of Gate and Front Streets, circa 1993**

The original Oban was built in 1822 and enlarged in the 1860s by Captain Milloy who operated the first steamship service to Toronto. It became a hotel in 1895 and was known as Oban House. A devastating fire destroyed the Oban on Christmas night 1992. It was exactingly reconstructed in 1993 and completed by the summer. Guests from the previous year who had to flee unfinished meals to escape the fire were invited to return to finish Christmas dinner in the summer!

Turn right on Front Street

**22. Golf Club, circa 1880s**

To your left is the clubhouse of the Niagara-on-the-Lake golf club, the oldest in Canada. The nine-hole course is built on the Fort Mississauga commons.

**23. Kirby House, 130 Front Street, circa 1818**

The Kirby House was the home of William Kirby, newspaper man, collector of customs for Niagara, novelist and early town historian. The house is another example of a frame building covered in roughcast to cut down on maintenance costs while giving the appearance of stone.

**24. Fort Niagara, Youngstown, N.Y., circa 1726**

Fort Niagara was built by the French, captured by the British, given to the Americans, recaptured by the British in 1813 and returned to the Americans at the end of the War of 1812. Today it is a beautifully preserved historic site. The cannons of this fort could reach Fort George, a little upriver from here. Where you are walking was in easy gunshot of the fort.

**25. Queen's Royal Park, circa 1866**

On this spot stood the luxurious Queen's Royal Hotel, the catalyst for Niagara's first tourism boom which ended with World War I. After the demolition of the hotel in the 1930s, the land was acquired by the town and has remained a public park.

**26. Bank of Upper Canada, 10 Front Street, circa 1817**

The Old Bank House is a frame building with a stucco front and rough-cast side treatment. As Niagara was being rebuilt after the War of 1812, the Bank of Upper Canada established a branch here. The money vaults have been preserved in the cellar of the house, now an historic Bed and Breakfast, one of dozens of beautifully maintained B&Bs in town.

Turn right on King Street.

**27. Masonic Hall, 153 King Street, circa 1816**

To the right is an early building reputedly constructed at the end of the War of 1812 from material salvaged from the burned town. The structure served several uses including a military barracks before becoming a Masonic Temple in the 1860s. Today it continues in use by the Freemasons while serving as the Chamber of Commerce office of the town.

**28. Preservation Gallery, 177 King Street, circa 1870s**

This large, beautifully restored house is a good example of the decorative style which marks the height of the Victorian age. The central tower and Saracen roof are notable features. The building serves as the gallery for the art of Trish Romance and is as splendid inside as are the exterior and gardens.

Turn right on Queen Street. The walker may choose to walk down either side of Queen to enjoy its historic stores.

### 29. *The Niagara Apothecary, 5 Queen Street, circa 1820*

The Apothecary building was a simple postwar structure until the 1850s when it was modified with the splendid italianate front preserved here today. This was an operating pharmacy for a century. It was one of the first buildings saved and restored through the efforts of the Niagara Foundation. It is refurnished to its Confederation period appearance with an selection of snake oil and cure-alls. A pharmacy museum is operated by the Ontario College of Pharmacy.

### 30. *The War Memorial Clock Tower, 1922*

In the middle of Queen Street is the tower built in 1922 as the town's War Memorial following World War I. It was rededicated after World War II to commemorate a new generation of Canadians who gave their lives for our freedom.

### 31. *Squire Clements Block, 4–8 Queen Street, circa 1835*

In the 1830s King Street was becoming busier while Queen was established as the main business street. This block has storefronts on Queen and one corner strorefront to attract shoppers from any direction.

### 32. *Firehall, 10 Queen Street, circa 1911*

This store was built by the Niagara fire brigade as their firehall in 1911. It has been commercial space for the past 8 decades.

### 33. *Loyalist Village, 12 Queen Street, circa 1850*

The store on this spot was built a few years after the completion of the courthouse, fell on hard times during the early 1860s but has been the site of thriving businesses for the past 120 years.

### 34. *Sign of the Pineapple, 16 Queen Street, circa 1830*

The well-restored building which houses The Owl and the Pussycat has interesting carved pineapples on window frame details and over the door. These were symbols of hospitality and welcome, sentiments still proudly upheld by the shop.

### 35. *Liquor Store, 20 Queen Street, circa 1817*

This extremely early brick building began as a one-storey structure. After the massive courthouse was completed in the 1840s, the building was expanded and a second storey added. It must be Ontario's most historic liquor store.

### 36. *Commercial Buildings, 7–9 Queen Street, circa 1890 and 1880*

Beside the Apothecary, these buildings were constructed as Niagara's first tourism boom got underway in the last decades of the nineteenth century. The styles are typical of commercial buildings in that time period and similar architecture can be seen in neighbouring Niagara-area towns.

### 37. *13–15 Queen Street, circa 1860*

A commercial block which some local historians feel may have been built as a residence is one of four buildings in the heritage district from the 1860s era. The early 1860s saw an economic downturn which slowed construction in the town.

### 38. *The Courthouse, 26 Queen Street, circa 1847*

This magnificent public building, a National Historic Site, was constructed as the county seat of the Niagara District with courtrooms, meeting rooms and jail cells. When the county seat was moved to St. Catharines in 1862, resulting in an economic downturn in Niagara, the courthouse became the town hall. It is also the site where the Shaw Festival was founded and it still houses the Court House Theatre of the Shaw. Notice the stone faces carved over the windows. Whether they are portraits of persons of the time or completely whimsical is not known.

### 39. *Sherlock Block, 34–36 Queen Street, circa 1850*

The Sherlock Block, actually two smaller buildings joined together, was contructed soon after the completion of the courthouse to take advantage of the many persons doing business at that building. The high façade conceals the fact that it is two buildings and gives the structure height to prevent it from being overwhelmed by the massive courthouse.

### 40. *The Irish Shop, 38–42 Queen Street, circa 1840*

Built during the height of the shipbuilding era partially as a shop and partially for residential space, this building like its neighbours on the block were originally built on land leased from the town.

### 41. *Old Niagara Bookshop, 44 Queen Street, circa 1981*

The bookshop and its neighbour, the Glens of Scotland, are in a restored building on the site of the Alma and Daly buildings. The stores are faithful copies of historic buildings.

**42. Bank of Commerce, 23–27 Queen Street, circa 1895**

A fire in the 1890s destroyed a block of buildings on this spot. Luckily, the blaze was brought under control before it could spread to surrounding wooden buildings. The present large brick structure was built to replace the burned stores in 1895.

Turn left on Regent Street and you have returned to the beginning of the tour.

# TOUR THREE
## *Biking Around Town*

This tour begins at the Fort George parking lot which is linked to the recreational bike path that extends all the way to Fort Erie. For this tour the cyclist proceeds across the Commons, a preserved natural area with a long history, past the site of the Indian Council House and Butler's Barracks to Mary Street where there is a bike lane. The route follows Mississauga Street, passes Fort Mississauga and then follows the waterfront to the dock area and along the Niagara River Parkway to John Street. Following the bike path along John the tour again crosses the Commons back to the start. In effect the route traces the perimeter of the old town past parks, military sites, the golf course and many historic houses. There are restaurants and a variety store en route for those who wish to stop for refreshments along the way. At the parking lot the tourism information centre has additional information on winery tours. Several of the wineries are close to the bike path along the parkway and others accessible by back roads.

From the Fort George parking lot, cross Queen's Parade to the recreational pathway across from the open fields of the Commons. This path is the Otter Trail, named after Sir William Otter, a Canadian military man.

**1. The Indian Council House, circa 1796**

Near the small bridge built by the Royal Canadian Engineers stood the Indian Council House, headquarters of the British Indian Department. At the time of the War of 1812, hundreds of Native people met here with British officials from time to time to discuss political issues.

**2. Butler's Barracks, circa 1816–1965**

The grey buildings are the remaining buildings of Butler's Barracks, an extensive collection of structures built to replace Fort George after the War of 1812. The new complex and surrounding fields became Camp Niagara where thousands of Canadian troops trained to fight in the Boer War, World War I, World War II and Korea.

Turn right and proceed on the path between the Butler's Barracks buildings. Cross King Street and continue on Mary.

**3. Brockamour, 433 King Street, circa 1818**

At the corner of King and Mary stands Brockamour House. Local legend claims that a daughter of the house, Sophia Shaw, was engaged to General Isaac Brock. After his death at the Battle of Queenston Heights, she never married. From time to time the ghost of Miss Shaw, quietly sobbing, is spotted in the halls of this magnificent place.

**4. Miller House, 46 Mary Street, circa 1817**

William Duff Miller built this house on the corner of Mary and Regent Streets. Miller was an officer of the Lincoln Militia, the coroner, county clerk and deputy clerk of crown and pleas. His house was conveniently located halfway between the business district and the Rye Street courthouse and within an easy stroll of Butler's Barracks.

**5. Little Africa**

The area bounded by Mary and Anne Streets and King and Mississauga Streets had many residents of African descent and became known as Little Africa. Some of the houses were among Niagara's most substantial structures while others were small structures patterned after the construction of slave cottages in the deep south of the United States. Many houses from the nineteenth century still stand in this area.

Turn right on Simcoe Street.

**6. Green House, 20 Simcoe Street, circa 1817–25**

The Green House started as a smaller home and eventually became a residential school, one of several operating in town at one point. It has been substantially altered and expanded during its long history.

**7. St. Andrews Presbyterian Church, Simcoe Street, circa 1821**

This distinctive brick church with its Greek Doric style portico and massive wooden pillars was restored in 1937.

It has an unusual orientation with the entrance leading past the pulpit. Peter Stokes observed that with such a lay-out there was "no sneaking into the back pew unnoticed."

### 8. Storington House, 289 Simcoe Street, circa 1817

The Storington House is built of brick and covered with stucco, one of the first houses built following the War of 1812. It was once the home of James Lockhart, one of the officers of the Niagara Harbour and Dock Company. It was a house for the well-to-do and contains a servants' loft for the hired help.

### 9. Butler House, 275 Simcoe Street, circa 1815

The Butlers were among the Loyalist founders of Niagara-on-the-Lake and this house was built on Mississauga Street by one of Colonel John Butler's sons. It was moved to this spot to prevent its demolition and has been restored to its 1815 appearance.

Continue on Simcoe and cross Queen Street.

### 10. Keily House, 209 Queen Street, circa 1832

The Keily Inn was built on the one piece of the Fort Mississauga commons which was not sold to the military by James Crooks in the 1820s. It was built for a lawyer, Charles Richardson who served Niagara as a member of parliament from 1832–34. The magnificent balconies were added in the late nineteenth century during the Niagara resort era. A very curious feature is a long vaulted chamber in the cellar, reputed to be a secret tunnel to Fort Mississauga.

### 11. Golf Course, circa 1880s

The Niagara-on-the-Lake Golf Club is the oldest in Canada. At one time, golfers played nine holes at Fort Mississauga and then proceeded to a nine-hole course near Fort George to finish the game. During World War I the Mississauga course was closed down while the commons here was used for training troops. The course was re-opened following World War I.

### 12. Fort Mississauga, circa 1814

The old fort with its massive brick and stone tower and unique star-shaped earthworks was built at the end of the War of 1812 along with Butler's Barracks to replace Fort George. The first few courses of the tower were constructed of brick salvaged from Ontario's first lighthouse which once stood here and from the ruins of the town, burned by

retreating enemy forces on December 10, 1813.

Turn right on Front Street.

### 13. Oban Inn, corner of Front and Gate Streets, circa 1993

The Oban is an accurate reconstruction of the original Oban Inn, built in 1822, destroyed by fire in 1992 and rebuilt the following year. During World War I, the inn served as the "mess," a combination club and dining room, for army officers training in Niagara.

### 14. Kirby House, 130 Front Street, circa 1818

William Kirby, the author of the first history of Niagara-on-the-Lake, novelist, collector of customs and newspaper man, lived in this old building, now restored.

### 15. Queen's Royal Park, circa 1866

On this spot stood the magnificent Queen's Royal Hotel which sparked Niagara's first tourism boom in the last part of the nineteenth century. Its tennis courts stood where the parking lot now sits. This is a great spot to view the river and Fort Niagara across the river mouth in Youngstown, New York.

Continue across King Street. Front Street is renamed Ricardo Street beyond King.

### 16. Dock area, foot of Melville Street

To your left is the dock area used from the early 1780s as a landing place. The ferry dock, Jet boat dock and marina are located in this area. The marina occupies one of the slips created for the Niagara Harbour and Dock Company. Many large steamboats were built in their yards.

### 17. Pumphouse Art Gallery, Ricardo Street, circa 1880s

The pumphouse was where the large engine which pumped water into the town was housed. The building has been restored and now operates as an art gallery where local art is displayed and lessons are offered.

### 18. Navy Hall, Ricardo Street, circa 1815

On this site, Lieutenant-Governor John Graves Simcoe established his residence and the offices of the Executive Council of Upper Canada in 1792. The buildings here were destroyed by cannon fire from the American shore in 1813. The current Navy Hall was built as a storeroom and barracks and is now used for meetings, banquets and wedding receptions. To your right are the ramparts of Fort George.

At Navy Hall, Ricardo Street becomes the Niagara River Parkway to Niagara Falls. Continue on this stretch to its junction with Queen's Parade. Continue straight across to link up with the bike path along John Street.

### 19. Brunswick Place, John Street, circa 1831

The Brunswick Place mansion was built for Captain Robert Melville, one of the founders of the Niagara Harbour and Dock company which brought prosperity to the town for a couple of decades during the first half of the nineteenth century. It was enlarged and embellished in the 1880s.

Continue along the path parallel with John Street and swing right to link up again with the Otter Trail. Continue back to Fort George.

### 20. Fort George, circa 1796

The old fort served as the headquarters of the British Army in Southern Ontario from 1796 until its capture by an American army in 1813, two days after it was largely destroyed by American cannon fire. The British re-occupied the fort in December 1813 but abandoned it after the war.

It was reconstructed in the 1930s. Today, the fort staff in 1812 period uniforms demonstrate life at the time of the war in the restored fort and its period refurnished buildings.

# *Appendix 2*
# SHAW FESTIVAL PRODUCTION HISTORY

## 1962

DON JUAN IN HELL
from MAN AND SUPERMAN
by Bernard Shaw

CANDIDA
by Bernard Shaw

## 1963

YOU NEVER CAN TELL
by Bernard Shaw

HOW HE LIED TO HER HUSBAND
by Bernard Shaw

THE MAN OF DESTINY
by Bernard Shaw

ANDROCLES AND THE LION
by Bernard Shaw

## 1964

HEARTBREAK HOUSE
by Bernard Shaw

VILLAGE WOOING
by Bernard Shaw

THE DARK LADY OF THE SONNETS
by Bernard Shaw

JOHN BULL'S OTHER ISLAND
by Bernard Shaw

## 1965

PYGMALION
by Bernard Shaw

THE SHADOW OF A GUNMAN
by Sean O'Casey

THE MILLIONAIRESS
by Bernard Shaw

## 1966

MAN AND SUPERMAN
by Bernard Shaw

MISALLIANCE
by Bernard Shaw

THE APPLE CART
by Bernard Shaw

# 1967

### ARMS AND THE MAN
by Bernard Shaw

### THE CIRCLE
by W. Somerset Maugham

### MAJOR BARBARA
by Bernard Shaw

# 1968

### HEARTBREAK HOUSE
by Bernard Shaw

### THE IMPORTANCE OF BEING OSCAR
based on the life and works of Oscar Wilde,
by Michael MacLiammoir

### THE CHEMMY CIRCLE
by Georges Feydeau

# 1969

### THE DOCTOR'S DILEMMA
by Bernard Shaw

### BACK TO METHUSALAH (Part I)
by Bernard Shaw

### THE GUARDSMAN
by Ferenc Molnar,
English version by Frank Marcu

# 1970

### CANDIDA
by Bernard Shaw

### FORTY YEARS ON
by Alan Bennett

# 1971

### THE PHILANDERER
by Bernard Shaw

### SUMMER DAYS
by Romain Weingarten,
translated by Suzanne Grossman

### TONIGHT AT 8:30
by Noel Coward

### "WAR, WOMEN AND OTHER TRIVIA"
### A SOCIAL SUCCESS
by Max Beerbohm

### O'FLAHERTY V.C.
by Bernard Shaw

### PRESS CUTTINGS
by Bernard Shaw

# 1972

### THE ROYAL FAMILY
by George S. Kaufman & Edna Ferber

### GETTING MARRIED
by Bernard Shaw

### MISALLIANCE
by Bernard Shaw

# 1973

### YOU NEVER CAN TELL
by Bernard Shaw

THE BRASS BUTTERFLY
by William Golding

FANNY'S FIRST PLAY
by Bernard Shaw

SISTERS OF MERCY: A MUSICAL JOURNEY
INTO THE WORDS OF LEONARD COHEN
conceived by Gene Lesser

## 1974

THE DEVIL'S DISCIPLE
by Bernard Shaw

THE ADMIRABLE BASHVILLE
by Bernard Shaw

TOO TRUE TO BE GOOD
by Bernard Shaw

CHARLEY'S AUNT
by Brandon Thomas

ROSMERSHOLM
by Henrik Ibsen

## 1975

PYGMALION
by Bernard Shaw

LEAVEN OF MALICE
by Robertson Davies

CAESAR AND CLEOPATRA
by Bernard Shaw

THE FIRST NIGHT OF PYGMALION
by Richard Huggett

G.K.C. — THE WIT AND WISDOM OF
GILBERT KEITH CHESTERTON
compiled, arranged and performed by Tony van Bridge

## 1976

THE ADMIRABLE CRICHTON
by J.M. Barrie

MRS WARREN'S PROFESSION
by Bernard Shaw

ARMS AND THE MAN
by Bernard Shaw

THE APPLE CART
by Bernard Shaw

## 1977

MAN AND SUPERMAN
by Bernard Shaw

THE MILLIONAIRESS
by Bernard Shaw

GREAT CATHERINE
by Bernard Shaw

WIDOWERS' HOUSES
by Bernard Shaw

THARK
by Ben Travers

## 1978

MAJOR BARBARA
by Bernard Shaw

JOHN GABRIEL BORKMAN
by Henrik Ibsen

HEARTBREAK HOUSE
by Bernard Shaw

LADY AUDLEY'S SECRET:
A MUSICAL MELODRAMA
by Mary Elizabeth Braddon,
adapted by Douglas Seale,
music by George Goehring,
lyrics by John Kuntz

## 1979

YOU NEVER CAN TELL
by Bernard Shaw

VILLAGE WOOING
by Bernard Shaw

CAPTAIN BRASSBOUND'S CONVERSION
by Bernard Shaw

DEAR LIAR
by Jerome Kilty

MY ASTONISHING SELF
from the writings of G.B.S.,
by Michael Voysey

THE CORN IS GREEN
by Emlyn Williams

BLITHE SPIRIT
by Noel Coward

## 1980

MISALLIANCE
by Bernard Shaw

THE CHERRY ORCHARD
by Anton Chekov

A FLEA IN HER EAR
by Georges Feydeau

THE GRAND HUNT
by Gyula Hernady

THE PHILANDERER
by Bernard Shaw

A RESPECTABLE WEDDING
by Bertolt Brecht,
translated by Jean Benedetti

CANUCK
by John Bruce Cowen

GUNGA HEATH
compiled and performed by Heath Lamberts

PUTTIN' ON THE RITZ
music and lyrics of Irving Berlin

OVERRULED
by Bernard Shaw

## 1981

SAINT JOAN
by Bernard Shaw

TONS OF MONEY
by Will Evans and Valentine

THE SUICIDE
by Nikolai Erdman

ROSE MARIE
book and lyrics by Otto Harbach and
Oscar Hammerstein II,
music by Rudolf Friml and Herbert Stothart

IN GOOD KING CHARLES'S GOLDEN DAYS
by Bernard Shaw

THE MAGISTRATE
by Arthur Wing Pinero

THE MAN OF DESTINY
by Bernard Shaw

CAMILLE
by Robert David MacDonald

## 1982

PYGMALION
by Bernard Shaw

THE DESERT SONG
book and lyrics by Otto Harbach,
Oscar Hammerstein II and Frank Mandel,
music adapted by Sigmund Romberg,
adapted by Christopher Newton

CAMILLE
by Robert David MacDonald

SEE HOW THEY RUN
by Philip King

THE MUSIC-CURE
by Bernard Shaw

TOO TRUE TO BE GOOD
by Bernard Shaw

THE SINGULAR LIFE OF ALBERT NOBBS
adapted by Simone Benmussa from *Albert Nobbs*,
by George Moore

CYRANO DE BERGERAC
by Edmond Rostand,
translated and adapted by Anthony Burgess

## 1983

CAESAR AND CLEOPATRA
by Bernard Shaw

CYRANO DE BERGERAC
by Edmond Rostand,
translated and adapted by Anthony Burgess

ROOKERY NOOK
by Ben Travers

TOM JONES
an operetta by Sir Edward German,
libretto by Robert Courtneidge and A.M. Thompson,
from the novel by Henry Fielding,
lyrics by Charles H. Taylor and Basil Hood,
libretto and lyrics adapted by Christopher Newton
and Sky Gilbert

THE SIMPLETON OF THE UNEXPECTED ISLES
by Bernard Shaw

CANDIDA
by Bernard Shaw

PRIVATE LIVES
by Noel Coward

O'FLAHERTY V.C.
by Bernard Shaw

THE VORTEX
by Noel Coward

# 1984

1984
by George Orwell,
adapted by Denise Coffey

THE DEVIL'S DISCIPLE
by Bernard Shaw

THE SKIN OF OUR TEETH
by Thornton Wilder

CELIMARE (or Friends of a Feather)
by Eugene Labiche,
adapted by Allan Stratton

ANDROCLES AND THE LION
by Bernard Shaw

PRIVATE LIVES
by Noel Coward

THE VORTEX
by Noel Coward

ROBERTA
books and lyrics by Otto Harbach,
music by Jerome Kern,
adapted by Duncan McIntosh and Christopher Newton

THE LOST LETTER
by Ian Luca Caragiale,
adapted by Christopher Newton and Sky Gilbert

"THE SHAW PLAYLETS":
THE FASCINATING FOUNDLING and
HOW HE LIED TO HER HUSBAND
by Bernard Shaw

# 1985

HEARTBREAK HOUSE
by Bernard Shaw

THE MADWOMAN OF CHAILLOT
by Jean Giraudoux,
adapted by Maurice Valency

NAUGHTY MARIETTA
book and lyrics by Rida Johnson Young,
music by Victor Herbert,
adapted by Christopher Newton

ONE FOR THE POT
by Ray Cooney and Tony Hilton

TROPICAL MADNESS NO. 2 —
METAPHYSICS OF A TWO-HEADED CALF
by Stanislaw Witkiewicz,
translated by Daniel and Eleanor Gerould

THE WOMEN
by Claire Booth Luce

JOHN BULL'S OTHER ISLAND
by Bernard Shaw

MURDER ON THE NILE
by Agatha Christie

THE INCA OF PERUSALEM
by Bernard Shaw

CAVALCADE
by Noel Coward

# 1986

BACK TO METHUSELAH (PARTS I AND II)
by Bernard Shaw

BLACK COFFEE
by Agatha Christie

BANANA RIDGE
by Ben Travers

ARMS AND THE MAN
by Bernard Shaw

CAVALCADE
by Noel Coward

ON THE ROCKS
by Bernard Shaw

HOLIDAY
by Philip Barry

GIRL CRAZY
music by George Gershwin,
lyrics by Ira Gershwin,
libretto by John McGowan and Guy Bolton

TONIGHT WE IMPROVISE
by Luigi Pirandello

PASSION, POISON AND PETRIFACTION
by Bernard Shaw

## 1987

HAY FEVER
by Noel Coward

MAJOR BARBARA
by Bernard Shaw

ANYTHING GOES
music and lyrics by Cole Porter,
book by Guy Bolton and P.G. Wodehouse,
revised by Howard Lindsay and Russell Crouse

MARATHON 33
by June Havoc

NOT IN THE BOOK
by Arthur Watkyn

FANNY'S FIRST PLAY
by Bernard Shaw

NIGHT OF JANUARY 16TH
by Ayn Rand

AUGUSTUS DOES HIS BIT
by Bernard Shaw

PETER PAN
by J.M. Barrie

PLAYING WITH FIRE
by August Stindberg

SALOME
by Oscar Wilde

## 1988

YOU NEVER CAN TELL
by Bernard Shaw

DANGEROUS CORNER
by J.B. Priestley

PETER PAN
by J.M. Barrie

HIT THE DECK
music by Vincent Youmans,
lyrics by Leo Robin, Clifford Grey and Irving Caesar,
book by Herbert Fields

GENEVA
by Bernard Shaw

WAR AND PEACE
by Leo Tolstoy,
adapted by Alfred Neumann,
Erwin Piscator and Guntram Pruefer,
translated by Robert David MacDonald

THE VOYSEY INHERITANCE
by Harley Granville Barker

THE DARK LADY OF THE SONNETS
by Bernard Shaw

ONCE IN A LIFETIME
by Moss Hart and George S. Kaufman

HE WHO GETS SLAPPED
by Leonid Andreyev

## 1989

MAN AND SUPERMAN
by Bernard Shaw

AN INSPECTOR CALLS
by J.B. Priestley

BERKELEY SQUARE
by John L. Balderston

ONCE IN A LIFETIME
by Moss Hart and George S. Kaufman

GOOD NEWS
music by Ray Henderson,
book by Laurence Schwab and B.G. DeSylva,
lyrics by B.G. DeSylva and Lew Brown

SHAKES VERSUS SHAV and
THE GLIMPSE OF REALITY
by Bernard Shaw

GETTING MARRIED
by Bernard Shaw

PEER GYNT
by Henrik Ibsen,
translated by John Lingard

TRELAWNY OF THE "WELLS"
by Arthur Wing Pinero

NYMPH ERRANT
music and lyrics by Cole Porter,
libretto by Romney Brent,
from the novel by James Laver

## 1990

MISALLIANCE
by Bernard Shaw

NYMPH ERRANT
music and lyrics by Cole Porter,
libretto by Romney Brent,
from the novel by James Laver

THE WALTZ OF THE TOREADORS
by Jean Anouilh,
translated by Lucienne Hill

NIGHT MUST FALL
by Emlyn Williams

TRELAWNY OF THE 'WELLS'
by Arthur Wing Pinero

MRS WARREN'S PROFESSION
by Bernard Shaw

WHEN WE ARE MARRIED
by J.B. Priestley

VILLAGE WOOING
by Bernard Shaw

PRESENT LAUGHTER
by Noel Coward

UBU REX
by Alfred Jarry, translated by David Copelin

## 1991

THE DOCTOR'S DILEMMA
by Bernard Shaw

LULU
by Frank Wedekind,
adapted by Peter Barnes

A CUCKOO IN THE NEST
by Ben Travers

THE MILLIONAIRESS
by Bernard Shaw

HENRY IV
by Luigi Pirandello

HEDDA GABLER
by Henrik Ibsen

A CONNECTICUT YANKEE
music by Richard Rodgers,
lyrics by Lorenz Hart,
book by Herbert Fields

THIS HAPPY BREED
by Noel Coward

PRESS CUTTINGS
by Bernard Shaw

## 1992

PYGMALION
by Bernard Shaw

COUNSELLOR-AT-LAW
by Elmer Rice

CHARLEY'S AUNT
by Brandon Thomas

WIDOWERS' HOUSES
by Bernard Shaw

DRUMS IN THE NIGHT
by Bertolt Brecht

POINT VALAINE
by Noel Coward

ON THE TOWN
music by Leonard Bernstein,
book and lyrics by Betty Comden and Adolph Green
based on an idea by Jerome Robbins

TEN MINUTE ALIBI
by Anthony Armstrong

OVERRULED
by Bernard Shaw

## 1993

SAINT JOAN
by Bernard Shaw

THE SILVER KING
by Henry Arthur Jones

BLITHE SPIRIT
by Noel Coward

CANDIDA
by Bernard Shaw

THE UNMENTIONABLES
by Carl Sternheim

THE MARRYING OF ANN LEETE
by Harley Granville Barker

GENTLEMEN PREFER BLONDES
music by Jule Styne
lyrics by Leo Robin
book by Anita Loos and Joseph Fields
adapted from the novel by Anita Loos

AND THEN THERE WERE NONE
by Agatha Christie

THE MAN OF DESTINY
by Bernard Shaw

## 1994

ARMS AND THE MAN
by Bernard Shaw

THE FRONT PAGE
by Ben Hecht and Charles MacArthur

SHERLOCK HOLMES
by William Gillette

TOO TRUE TO BE GOOD
by Bernard Shaw

EDEN END
by J.B. Priestley

IVONA, PRINCESS OF BURGUNDIA
by Witold Gombrowicz

LADY, BE GOOD!
music and lyrics by
George Gershwin and Ira Gershwin
book by Guy Bolton and Fred Thompson

BUSMAN'S HONEYMOON
by Dorothy L. Sayers

ROCOCO
by Harley Granville Barker

ANNAJANSKA, THE BOLSHEVIK EMPRESS
by Bernard Shaw

## 1995

YOU NEVER CAN TELL
by Bernard Shaw

THE PETRIFIED FOREST
by Robert E. Sherwood

CAVALCADE
by Noel Coward

THE PHILANDERER
by Bernard Shaw

AN IDEAL HUSBAND
by Oscar Wilde

WASTE
by Harley Granville Barker

THE VOICE OF THE TURTLE
by John van Druten

LADIES IN RETIREMENT
by Edward Percy

THE ZOO
by Arthur Sullivan and Bolton Rowe

THE SIX OF CALAIS
by Bernard Shaw

## 1996

THE DEVIL'S DISCIPLE
by Bernard Shaw

RASHOMON
by Fay and Michael Kanin

HOBSON'S CHOICE
by Harold Brighouse

AN IDEAL HUSBAND
by Oscar Wilde

THE SIMPLETON OF THE UNEXPECTED ISLES
by Bernard Shaw

THE PLAYBOY OF THE WESTERN WORLD
by J.M. Synge

MARSH HAY
by Merrill Denison

MR. CINDERS
music by Vivian Ellis and Richard Myers
libretto and lyrics by Clifford Grey and
Greatrex Newman
additional lyrics by Leo Robin and Vivian Ellis

THE HOLLOW
by Agatha Christie

SHALL WE JOIN THE LADIES?
by J.M. Barrie

THE CONJUROR
by Patrick Watson and David Ben

LUNCHTIME READING SERIES:
*Murder Pattern* by Herman Voaden
*War of the Worlds* by Howard Koch
*Farfetched Fables* by Bernard Shaw
*To Have and to Hold* by Jules Renard

## 1997

MRS. WARREN'S PROFESSION
by Bernard Shaw

HOBSON'S CHOICE
by Harold Brighouse

WILL ANY GENTLEMAN?
by Vernon Sylvaine

THE SEAGULL
by Anton Chekhov

IN GOOD KING CHARLES'S GOLDEN DAYS
by Bernard Shaw

THE PLAYBOY OF THE WESTERN WORLD
by J.M. Synge

THE CHILDREN'S HOUR
by Lillian Hellman

THE SECRET LIFE
by Harley Granville Barker

THE CHOCOLATE SOLDIER
music by Oscar Straus

THE TWO MRS. CARROLLS
by Martin Vale

THE CONJUROR (PART 2)
by David Ben and Patrick Watson

SORRY, WRONG NUMBER
by Lucille Fletcher

BELL CANADA READING SERIES:
*Why She Would Not* by Bernard Shaw
*The Intruder* by Maurice Maeterlinck
*Still Stands the House* by Gwen Pharis Ringwood
*The Titanic* by E.J. Pratt

# 1998

**MAJOR BARBARA**
by Bernard Shaw

**YOU CAN'T TAKE IT WITH YOU**
by George S. Kaufman and Moss Hart

**LADY WINDERMERE'S FAN**
by Oscar Wilde

**THE LADY'S NOT FOR BURNING**
by Christopher Fry

**JOHN BULL'S OTHER ISLAND**
by Bernard Shaw

**JOY**
by John Galsworthy

**A FOGGY DAY**
words and music by George and Ira Gershwin

**THE SHOP AT SLY CORNER**
by Edward Percy

**PASSION, POISON AND PETRIFACTION**
by Bernard Shaw

**BROTHERS IN ARMS**
by Merrill Denison

**WATERLOO**
by Arthur Conan Doyle

**BELL CANADA READING SERIES**
*Trifles* by Susan Glaspell
*Shavian Scrapbook* by Bernard Shaw
*The Ballad of Reading Gaol* by Oscar Wilde
*A Drink with Adolphus* by Ethel Wilson

# 1999

**HEARTBREAK HOUSE**
by Bernard Shaw

**YOU CAN'T TAKE IT WITH YOU**
by George S. Kaufman and Moss Hart

**EASY VIRTUE**
by Noel Coward

**ALL MY SONS**
by Arthur Miller

**GETTING MARRIED**
by Bernard Shaw

**THE MADRAS HOUSE**
by Harley Granville Barker

**S.S. TENACITY**
by Charles Vildrac

**UNCLE VANYA**
by Anton Chekhov

**REBECCA**
by Daphne du Maurier

**A FOGGY DAY**
words and music by George and Ira Gershwin

**WATERLOO**
by Arthur Conan Doyle

**VILLAGE WOOING**
by Bernard Shaw

**BELL CANADA READING SERIES**
*The Adventures of the Black Girl in Her Search for God* by Bernard Shaw
*Lessons from Leacock* by Stephen Leacock
*The Apollo of Bellac* by Jean Giraudoux
*The Birds* by Daphne du Maurier

# BIBLIOGRAPHY

Niagara-on-the-Lake has a fascinating museum, preserved historic sites and plaques and a very well-equipped research centre in the Public Library, where one can learn much more about the historic town.

The following sources are suggested for those wishing to delve a little further into Niagara-on-the-Lake's story.

## Architectural History

Butler, Nancy. Unpublished files collected over years of research. (Private Collection)

Field, John L. *Niagara-on-the-Lake Guidebook.* Niagara Falls, Ont.: Renown Printing, 1984.

Mika, Helma, and Nick Mika (with Nancy Butler and Joy Ormsby). *Niagara-on-the-Lake: the Old Historical Town.* Belleville, Ont.: Mika Publishing, 1990.

Stokes, Peter John. *Old Niagara-on-the-Lake.* Toronto: University of Toronto Press, 1971.

## The Shaw Festival

Doherty, Brian. *Not Bloody Likely: The Shaw Festival: 1962–1973.* Toronto: J.M. Dent and Sons, 1974.

Garebian, Keith. *George Bernard Shaw and Christopher Newton: Explorations of Shavian Theatre.* Oakville, Ont.: Mosaic Press, 1993.

Holmes, Katherine, ed. *Celebrating! Twenty-Five Years on the Stage at the Shaw Festival.* Erin, Ont.: Boston Mills Press, 1986.

Newton, Christopher. *Shaw Festival Handbook,* published annually by the Shaw Festival.

## General History of the Town

Carnochan, Janet. *History of Niagara.* Belleville, Ont.: Mika Publishing, 1973 (originally published in 1914).

Field, John L., ed. *Bicentennial Stories of Niagara-on-the-Lake.* Lincoln, Ont.: Rannie Publications, 1981.

Habermehl, Fred, and Donald L. Combe. *Stones, Saints and Sinners: Walking Tours of Niagara-on-the-Lake's Large Historic Cemeteries.* Niagara-on-the-Lake: Niagara Historical Society, 1995.

Innis, Mary Quayle, ed. *Mrs Simcoe's Diary.* Toronto: Macmillan, 1965.

Kirby, William. *Annals of Niagara.* Niagara Falls, Ont.: Lundy's Lane Historical Society, 1972 (originally published 1896).

Merritt, Richard, Nancy Butler and Michael Power, eds. *The Capital Years: Niagara-on-the-Lake, 1792-1796*. Niagara-on-the-Lake: Niagara Historical Society, 1991.

Niagara-on-the-Lake Bicentennial Committee. *Niagara-on-the-Lake, 1781-1981*. Niagara-on-the-Lake: Acton Press, 1981.

Power, Michael, and Nancy Butler. *Slavery and Freedom in Niagara*. Niagara-on-the-Lake: Niagara Historical Society, 1993.

Walker, Susan, and Dori Herod. *Exploring Niagara-on-the-Lake and the Niagara Peninsula*. Toronto: Greey de Pencier Publications, 1977.

## Military History

While many excellent publications relating the history of the Niagara Region have recently been written, an in-depth account of the military history of Niagara can be found in a remarkable collection of documents filling almost 2,000 volumes in the National Archives of Canada, R.G. 8, Military "C" Series.

# ACKNOWLEDGEMENTS

The task of preparing a summary of the rich and complex history of Niagara-on-the-Lake was a labour of love which was made considerably easier with the help of friends.

I am grateful to Nancy Butler of Niagara-on-the-Lake for lending research material and steering me towards other sources and to town historian Joy Ormsby, Parks Canada Pre-history Archaeologist Brian Ross and Shaw Festival historian Denis Johnston for reading the manuscript and offering further information and advice. The Niagara-on-the-Lake library contains a good collection of books and documents on Niagara and I thank Gerda Molson and staff for their assistance. I appreciate the hard work of Carolin Muise, Assistant Curator of the Niagara Historical Society Museum for tracking down paintings and photos of early Niagara-on-the-Lake from the museum's extensive collection. I also thank Bill Severin, Curator of the museum for his insightful conversations with me on the history of the town. James Campbell of the Weir Gallery gave me free access to that gallery's impressive collection of early Canadiana and helped choose some beautiful paintings for reproduction in this book as did Brian Dunnigan of the University of Michigan. John Burtniak, the knowledgeable librarian of the library's special collections at Brock University put a large personal collection of postcards of Niagara at my disposal. Ronald Williamson of Archaeological Services Inc., who has done so much work in uncovering the prehistoric past in the Niagara Peninsula, freely shared photos and images from his collection. Odette Yazbeck of the Shaw Festival provided a super collection of slides documenting the theatre's offerings over the years. I would also like to thank Parks Canada colleagues Brian Morin, Derek Cooke and Rosemary Campbell for access to the Parks Canada collections. Niagara-on-the-Lake's Recreation Director Clive Buist lent photos of the town in full bloom. I am most grateful to Christopher Newton, the incomparable Artistic Director of the Shaw, not only for his foreword to this book but for the years that he has dedicated to making Niagara-on-the-Lake the cultural and heritage paradise that it has become. Thanks also to the Shaw's Administrative Director Colleen Blake.

Encouragement during this project came from a variety of my associates on the Chamber of Commerce, Niagara Foundation, Friends of Fort George, Niagara National Historic Sites and TEMCO. Inspiration came from the town itself and from the wonderful people who live here, most of whom appreciate the town's rich past and strive to preserve it.

Finally I would like to thank my wife Nancy who read and re-read chapter drafts and made valuable suggestions on the flow of the narrative.

# INDEX

## Photo Credits

Key: T = Top, C = Centre, B = Bottom

Images on the following pages appear courtesy of the individuals and institutions noted below. All other photographs were taken by Dwayne Coon and are the property of the publisher.

Archaeology Services Inc.: 21, 22, 24, 25;  Archives of Ontario: 31T (S-1439); Brock University Library: 42, 43T, 44, 45, 46, 48; Cooper, David: 64, 65; Dale, Ron: 32, 46, 47; Metropolitan Toronto Reference Library: 23, 27B, 37B, 38; Niagara-on-the-Lake Historical Society: 40; National Archives of Canada: 27T (C-042572), 33 (C-012094), 43B (C-0l8737); Parks Canada: 6, 26B, 29, 31B; Shaw Festival: 60, 61(Gordon More), 62, 63 (Robert C. Ragsdale): The Weir Foundation: 30, 36; William L. Clements Library: 26T, 28 (198C)
Maps: McKowen, Scott: 9; Daly, Tim: 10